AF480114

JAIME MOYER

FEARLESS OVER FAILURE

DEDICATION

To my parents, James & Sharon
Thank you for raising me with the love and discipline
necessary to get me to where I am in life today. Thank
you for never giving up on me even when I'd push you to
your limits and test your patients. Thank you for always
believing in me and encouraging me to do my best and to
follow my dreams with dedication and determination.

To the my Lord and Savior Jesus Christ
Thank you for answering my prayers to keep me
dedicated and motivated in the writing process of this
book. And for giving me the content for this book and the
words to say in each chapter to make this book possible.

To all those who read this book
Thank you for taking the time to read this book about my
life. I truly hope you enjoy it and find inspiration from the
things I've endured in my life thus far. Remember, Take
NOTHING for granted and be true to your self no matter
what anybody else think or tells you. Again thank you for
reading this book and God Bless You!

CONTENTS

Introduction: Intro Into My Life 7

Chapter 1: Birth / Childhood 11

Chapter 2: "The Bad Kid" 16

Chapter 3: Troubled Teen 22

Chapter 4: Drugs And Alcohol 32

Chapter 5: Caught In The Middle 42

Chapter 6: Shattered Dreams 54

Chapter 7: Mental Heath Matters 67

Chapter 8: "Don't Let Me Die!" 81

Chapter 9: Jesus Is My Savior, Not My Religion...... 93

Chapter 10: Sobriety, Recovery and Relapse 105

Chapter 11: Becoming A Christian 115

Epilogue: Living Fearlessly 125

INTRO INTO MY LIFE

I am one of two children to my dad and one of three children to my mom. I am the oldest of my dads children and the middle child to my mom. My brother Philip who is technically my half brother, same mom with different dads, is two years older then me. My sister and I were raised not to view him as our half brother or step brother so we always just referred to him as our brother. He's one heck of a fighter as he was born with Cerebral Palsy and later in life, in his 20's was

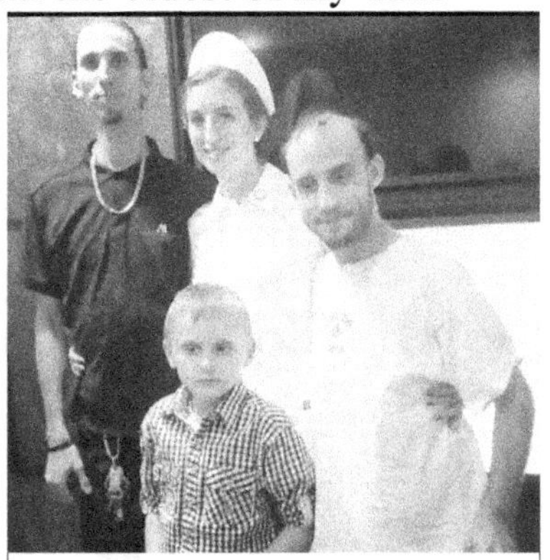

Left to Right: Me, Adrienne (sister), Philip (brother)
Front: Zach (cousin)

diagnosed with the Progressive stages of Multiple Sclerosis.

I love my brother and couldn't imagine life without him although I know due to his health issues life without him will inevitably happen sooner rather then later. I remember when we were kids and those bicycle chain necklaces were the cool thing to have, My brother had one and we were rough housing one day. Needless to say I broke it and boy did he ever get mad. When I tell you it was like the Lord performed a miracle and gave him the ability to walk normally just so he could put me in a choke hold and damn near choke me out before mom had to intervene, I promise you can't make that kind of thing up.

My sister Adrienne is a year younger then me. She probably the most normal one out of us kids although sometimes she makes me wonder but I love her to death. She made me an uncle to two little nephew who I will talk more about the oldest one later in this book. We didn't grow up with a lot of money so my sister and I shared a room for basically our entire lives growing up which I know what your thinking, "That's really weird dude!" And though to a point it was somewhat, It taught us boundaries and privacy.

I remember one night when we were young there was this news story about this man who was going around town abducting kids and my sister got so scared she refused to go to sleep. I got so mad that she wouldn't go to sleep that I helped her round up literally every hard and or blunt object in our room, Everything from baseball bats to pieces of wood to toys to skateboards, literally EVERYTHING and ANYTHING we could find to cause harm to a human being with and split it between us just in case this man broke into our room, which was on the second floor of an apartment, just so my sister would go to sleep. Heck I even had a sling shot my dad got me from Christmas I believe it was the year before. Only then did my sister finally go to sleep and it was a school night and by this time it had to be about midnight. I have so many stories about growing up with my sister it's not even funny. But I wouldn't trade any of them for the world.

As for me, I'm just your typical, average guy. Not much special about me, I enjoy drawing, video games, skateboarding, sports and pretty much anything that gives me a reason to be outdoors. I play softball for my churches Softball team, I play Catcher for the most part and occasionally a little bit of Right Field. I began playing Softball in 2013 for the church I attended at that time Grace Fellowship Church of Ephrata where I also played Catcher and Right Field and I played on that team until 2017. I took 2018 and 2019 off from playing as the church no longer had a team after 2017 and then I began attending Reamstown Church Of God in 2020 after their softball season where they won the Championship. The next year I joined the team and am still currently playing.

Grace Fellowship Church of Ephrata 2017 Softball Team

I also enjoy Skateboarding, which I got from my dad. One of my fondest memories as a kid is watching my dad tear around town on his skateboard. He had this purplish Vision skateboard with neon green wheels. My parents got me a skateboard when I was a kid and I was never very good at doing tricks and stuff but I could do a pretty respectable Ollie as a kid. Of course my parents started me out on a Walmart board, Had to prove I could take care of that before they'd buy me a real nice board.

Another love of mine is drawing, I began to love art class in elementary school and then in middle school became even more interested in drawing. I even started entering my drawing into the local fair year after year and rarely ever did I not walk away with a placement ribbon. My favorite artist is Georgia O'Keeffe and my favorite of her art is her New Mexico Era of art. Fun Fact I went to the same college as her, Only I attended The Art Institute Of York – Pennsylvania and she attended The Art Institute of Chicago. I went to college for art which we will get into more later on in this book. Lets just say those were some of the best and worst times of my life.

Chapter 1

BIRTH | CHILDHOOD

"Before I formed you in the womb, I knew you.
Before you were born I set you apart."
- Jeremiah 1:5

I was born October 24th, 1990 at 10:51am at the Lancaster General Hospital in Lancaster, Pennsylvania to my parents James, Jim for short, and Sharon. My original due date was November 25th, 1990 so I was born an entire month early making me a premature baby. If that wasn't enough I kept trying to turn around and come out feet first out of my mothers womb, The doctor had to keep turning me head first in which I'd turn right back to feet first. Beings I was born prematurely I was put into the Neonatal Intensive Care Unit, the NICU for short, at the hospital. This is the part of the hospital where if your basically not a relative of the baby, you don't get to enter.

One day when I was in the NICU my fathers parents came in to visit and my grandpa noticed the baby next to me in the NICU was shaking very much and had asked the nurse, why the baby was shaking so much? The nurse said to him that the mother had smoked crack while she was pregnant so now the baby was going through symptoms of withdraw. After I was discharged from the hospital and my mother and father were able to bring me home I came home to our apartment in Reinholds,

Pennsylvania where my mother and father lived in one of the two second floor apartments. Below our apartment lived my mothers parents, my grandparents as well as my brother. At this time I was my dads only child and my mothers second child, my sister wouldn't come into the picture until about a year and a half later.

I was a pretty wild child to say the least. If trying to come out of the womb butt first wasn't funny enough, I remember my mother telling me a story about how as a child I refused to crawl. Instead I would slide around on my back and I would use the heels of my feet to scoot around. Now as funny as that sounds this next part isn't so funny. Because of that I ended up getting this quarter sized blisters on the heel of my one foot and my grandpa had to pop it. I know your probably thinking, "Wow, That's gross" but could you imagine how painful that had to be for ME?

When I turned 3 years old I had my first seizure. Seizures ran in the family on my mothers side as my mother, my brother, my uncle, my aunt and my grandma all on my mothers side of the family suffered from Seizure Disorders. My brother has what they refer to as grand-male seizures which are the ones everyone thinks of when you hear about seizures. They are the ones where they say you can "swallow your tongue" so its important to make sure the person tongue is secured so they don't swallow it. Two things which are not true by the way, It's actually physically impossible to literally swallow your tongue and you should NEVER put ANYTHING inside the mouth of a parson having a seizure as it causing a choking hazard for the person having the seizure. If anything you should turn the person over on they're side so that the saliva and any other gunk in their mouth can exit their mouth and you should call 911 immediately.

Anyway, Back to me and my Seizure Disorder. I have what they call acute seizures which basically means

I stare off into space and I convulse uncontrollably. This usually last anywhere from a few seconds to a couple minutes and if it lasts for 5 minutes or more, You should call 911 if you haven't done so already. The most important thing to remember when someone is having a seizure is don't freak out. Because when you freak out your aren't able to think clearly and then you will be unable to be of help to the person having the seizure. Even to this day I still take medication for my Seizure Disorder and see a Neurologist to help manage my Seizure Disorder.

Also when I was 3 years old my mother started taking me to church on a regular bases. My father didn't attend with us due to the fact that he worked construction and the weekends were his days off work so he would sleep in and relax on those days. My mother took us to a church in Ephrata, Pennsylvania called Grace Fellowship Church of Ephrata. As long as I can remember going to church was a must growing up, Unless we were legitimately sick we went to church. We even attended church on Wednesdays as I got a little older and was old enough to take part in the AWANA program at church. My mother was even a teacher in the AWANA program for the Cubbies. Though when our church started that program I was told old for Cubbies and started at a higher level in the program.

My mother making attending church such a important aspect of my childhood would later pay off as when I was 5 years old I was in the car with my mother and my brother. I don't remember much other then that this moment lead to me asking the Lord to come into my life and be my Savior. Looking back on this moment now I feel like I only did so because I knew it was the right thing to do and that I didn't quite understand what I was doing at the time. Later in my life when I was 10 years old I would make the decision to be baptized by water at church. I remember that very well, The Pastor at the time would be the one to baptize me. Pastor would pass away in 2022 and of course him baptizing me is one of the most treasured memories I have of him.

At the age of 8 years old I would be diagnosed with Attention Deficit Disorder, A.D.D for short. My teacher in elementary school at the time would be the one who noticed my lack of focus in school and my lack of being able to sit still and would reach out to my parents with the concern that I may have Attention Deficit Disorder. My mother would take me to the doctor and he had confirmed that I indeed has Attention Deficit Disorder and would place me on medication for it. This would change my education as now I would be given an Individualized Education Program, IEP for short, to help me to succeed in school and help the teachers better educate me. This would also come with a price to pay as the not so nice kids in school would use this as an opportunity to pick on me. This would last the rest of my time in elementary school all the way till I graduated high school.

My Attention Deficit Disorder wasn't the only thing that the kids would pick on me for. My parents raised me the best they could and they did a good job doing so with the little money they had. Dad was a construction worker and Mom worked in a factory and later went into food service. Mom didn't make much money so Dads income paid a good majority of the bills. So of course my school supplies my parents tried their absolute hardest to get us the coolest backpacks and binders and cloths and what not that they could but of course they could really afford the Aeropostle and Ambercombie And Fitch, etc that all the "cool kids" had so we had to settle for Walmart. When the other kids would see this, They'd of course make fun of me for being poor or for having no money.

      My teeth were also kind of crooked and what not so the kids would pick on me for that as my parents could afford to get me braces. And I'm kind of glad they didn't because then the kids would've just pick on me for have braces. The kids were really mean in school, If making fun of my appearance and parents not having much money wasn't bad enough they'd shove me in lockers. All these things would make me angry and I'd fire back telling them to shut up or by pushing or hitting them which never seemed to work out in my favor. They'd either push and hit me back or the teacher always seemed to come along when I was the one doing the hitting or pushing so then I'd get in trouble. They say if your being bullied tell somebody but what they fail to realize is that either gets you bullied

Picture of me when I was little, I believe this was from Cub Scouts

even more or if your like me whoever you tell never believes you and always believes the kids who are bullying you.

      Also my mom introducing me to church has played a major role in my life. Later on in this book I was speak more on that and go into greater detail about how that has effected my life and the things it has done for me. Without my mother introducing me to church I don't know if I'd even be alive to day as that's another topic we will dive into later on in this book. So you definitely going to want to stay tuned as I promise this book just keeps getting better and better. My childhood wasn't easy but I don't regret a single moment of it and I'm thankful for the life my parents provided me with. My parents are to this day two of the most influential people in my life and I couldn't image the day they are no longer here.

Chapter 2

"THE BAD KID"

"Do not be deceived;
Bad company ruins good morals"
- 1 Corinthians 15:33

Outside of school I wasn't able to play with the kids in town much because I was know as "the bad kid." I was the kid you told your kids to stay away from because I were "bed news." I did however have two good friends as a young kid. One was named Tyler and the other was named Josh. Tyler lived about two or three blocks away and Josh lived about a mile or two away and was the son of my moms friend. Tyler had an older sister name Rachel who would occasionally hang out with us and Josh had like five siblings of which his two brothers Ben and Daniel, Danny for short, would occasionally hang out with us as well.

Tyler came from a not so healthy home. His mom was living with a guy who wasn't Tyler's dad so Tyler would not listen to him and often back talk him when I was over. He'd tell his moms boyfriend things like, "Shut up your not my dad" or "I don't have to listen to you" things like that. We usually spent our time together playing Tony Hawk Pro Skater on PlayStation and if we weren't doing that we were outside Skateboarding in the lumber yard next to my house. His sister would even come skateboarding with us sometimes. I remember my brother had the BIGGEST crush on Rachel and I swear if memory serves me correctly they even did end up dating for a little bit.

Tyler and Josh were both in my grade in school, Tyler ended up even being in my homeroom class in the fifth grade. This would serve to end up being trouble as I enjoyed drawing and I was also quite impressionable. Tyler use to like to draw pigs so I started drawing pigs as well. One day in homeroom our teacher let us have some free time and it was the day after the Daytona 500 where Dale Earnhardt Sr tragically lost his life in a wreck on the last lap. I don't know why I thought this was a good idea but I decided to draw a picture of the ginger bread man eating Dale Earnhardt Sr's car with him in it. I showed it to Tyler and he dared me to put curse words on it.

So I did, I put some speech bubbles with curse words in them. My teacher came along as saw it and boy did I get in trouble. She yelled at me and made me take it home and show my mother. I had to return to school the next day with said picture with my mothers signature on it so my teacher knew my mother saw it. Luckily my mother was on my side on this one as she called the teacher and asked the teacher why she would tell a bunch of fifth graders to do "whatever they wanted to." The next day I returned to school with the picture and gave it to my teacher so she could see I showed it to my mom.

The teacher would then tell me that I had to stay in from recces for an entire week as punishment. I told Tyler about what happened and we would come up with a clever nickname for our teacher Mrs. Eidemiller. We would refer to her as Mrs. Eidekiller and in an annoying nagging voice say, "In for a week, In for a week, In In In In for a week." We'd of course never do this when she was around so she had no clue about it but it still is quite funny to this day. Tyler would eventually move away as his mom broke up with her boyfriend and they moved not to far away but then moved again and I lost contact with Tyler. I still wonder to this day what he's up to and where he is.

Tyler and I even went to this youth group called Crossfire Youth Ministries. I was the coolest place ever, The guy who ran it would even pick you up at your house in a big blue school bus. I eventually invited Tyler and he came along and we would spend our time there skateboarding with the other kids who skateboarded there. This was also the time putting literal screws in your ears as earrings was the cool thing to do and Tyler did so. The thing about this youth group was we would often have pillow fights as there were couches everywhere which meant pillows everywhere. I remember someone hit Tyler in the side of the head with pillow and next thing I know I heard Tyler scream as blood poured from his ear.

The person who had hit Tyler with the pillow hadn't realized the pillow got caught on the screw in Tyler's ear and when they pulled the pillow away it ripped the screw out of Tyler's ear and ripped his ear lobe in half. I never seen so much blood in my life. Crossfire was the coolest youth group ever they had a snack bar you could buy candy and sodas at, they had video games, and of course literally anyone and everyone young enough went there. Yes even the bullies from school some of them went there as well which tended to get me into some trouble as being bullied at school would occasionally spill into being bullied at youth group. And when you got a hundred or so kids running around it don,t matter how many adults you got around they're not gonna see everything that happens. I attended Crossfire until I was to old to attend anymore, which was 18 years old.

Now back to Josh, Josh was so cool. He was smaller then me so he was really fast. Id come home from school and tell my mom who was usually on the phone with Josh's mom that I was going to Josh's house. So she'd tell Josh's mom Bonnie that I'd be over shortly. Josh's mom Bonnie and dad Andy where so awesome and always greeted me with a hello. Josh's house had the biggest yard I've ever seen in my life with the biggest tree I've ever seen in my life with the longest rope swing I'd ever seen in my life.

Josh also had this annoying little yippy dog named Patches. We use to be so mean to that dog. Josh and I both like Professional Wrestling so we use to take Patches and throw him on the bed and elbow drop him and stuff. Looking back on it now that was absolutely terrible and no wonder that dog would randomly try to bite your ankle for no good reason and was scared of everything that moved. Josh also had this big shaggy brown dog named Teddy. That dog looked like a giant teddy bear and literally was the coolest looking dog ever.

Later in life Josh's family would get this big black dog name Jessie, I HATED Jessie. This dog had the loudest most intimidating bark ever and would bark at everyone who came to the house. I was a teenager at the time and this dog chased me up the stairs and had me crawling on top of the bunk bed yelling, screaming and crying my teenage eyes out as he was at the bottom barking his head off with pure evil in his eyes. Josh's sister would babysit me at their house so I spent a good bit of my childhood at Josh's house between being babysat and just hanging out their with Josh and his siblings to play. Josh's grandpa even lived at the house and he was so cool his name was Jack but I never called him Jack, I'd call him grandpa even though he wasn't my grandpa.

I invited Josh to AWANA's when I was a kid and he came. He liked it so he came more and more, I believe his brother Ben might have came eventually as well. After we got to old for AWANA's we went into the youth group and I remember we use to go to Schroon Lake, New York at the Word Of Life Bible Institute every year for Snow Camp. They had competitions between all the attending churches, Things like Basketball, Volleyball, Soccer, Dodge ball, and even the infamous Cardboard Sled Race. Josh was always so good at the competitions. It was almost insane how good he was.

I remember one year during Dodge ball he jumped so high to avoid being hit with the dodge ball and it ended up hitting him square in the jewels. Everyone was like, "Oooooooooooh," Needless to say that didn't count as him being out. But the funny part was at the end of the week they'd show a Week In Review video and Josh getting hit in the jewels was highlighted on the video. Another thing I remember about Snow Camp with Josh is he played a prank on me once where he put my sleeping bag out in the snow. Now this is New York there isn't like an inch or two of snow, No this was like a half foot of snow if not more so my sleeping bag was soaked with no way to dry it other then to let it air dry. I was so mad at him and at the time it wasn't very funny but looking back at it now it was kind of hilarious.

The same youth group where we attended Snow Camp was actually the same youth group I'd end up meeting another friend who to this day is still my friend. In fact It's safe to say we are best friends. And his name is Jared and he and I have done literally everything together. So much that I'll get into more about us and our friendship later on in this book. Jared and I have become so good friends that his family is like my family and my family is like his family. Jared and my friends is so wild that you might want to buckle up because it gets to be quite the bumpy road later on in life.

If there's one thing my childhood has taught me it is that life isn't fair, and to value the friendship in your life because you don't know how long they last. And if they do last a long time your friendship can become more like a brotherhood if you play your cards right. I've also learned two wrongs don't make a right. Especially when it comes to someone picking on you and bullying you. I wouldn't trade any of the friendships I had as a kid for the world and each and everyone of them has helped me get to where I am today.

Chapter 3

TROUBLED TEEN

*"Whoever will not observe the law of your God
and the law of the king, let judgment be executed
upon him strictly, whether for death or for banishment
or for confiscation of goods or for imprisonment."*
- Ezra 7:26

All though out my years in school I was constantly in and out of detention and suspension as a result of my behavior. Most of the time it stemmed from me defending myself against a bully in the wrong way by taking matters into my own hand. Once I got into high school that's when the real trouble began. That's when I would find out what the back of a police car looked like. That's when I'd find out about the District Justice and the consequences of acting out as a juvenile. This is when I'd drive my parents the most crazy.

When I was 15 years old I would begin smoking cigarettes. I would hang out with this kid Brandon who lived up the road from me and we would go down to the lumber yard when they closed and fish through the ash trays outside for cigarette butts that still had some tobacco left in them. We'd take all the cigarettes and roll them into new full pre made cigarettes. I know again your probably thinking, " Dude, That's so gross, Who does that!" But when your 15 years old and not old enough to buy cigarettes but want to look cool by smoking cigarettes with your friends who also smoke, You'll do just about anything to get your hands on cigarettes. Even if it means enjoying sloppy seconds from a cigarette that was in someone else mouth.

After school one day Brandon and I were outside my house and my house had still had the Halloween decorations up. It was a week or two after Halloween and my mom just hadn't gotten around to taking them down. We had this plastic skeleton hanging on the front door of our apartment. Brandon and I were sitting on the wall getting ready to smoke but Brandon realized he forgot his lighter at home, Or so I thought. He went home to "get his lighter" and I waited outside my house on the wall for him to come back. Next thing I knew I heard my mom screaming so I turned around to see the plastic skeleton on our front door half melted on fire and Brandon nowhere to be found.

By this time my mom had already called the police and I was the only one around when they got there. After that I had to go to the District Justice who charged me with arson and gave me a fine to pay as well as a hundred hours of community service to complete. My mom ended up paying the fine for me but as for the one hundred hours of community service I was stuck to do that myself. I ended up doing my community service at a local church mowing the yard and weeding the gardens. I eventually completed my one hundred hours of community service and I never hung out with Brandon again. Our friendship was over at that point.

A little over a year later when I was 16 years old I would find myself in trouble with the law again only this time it was for harassment. My dad had bought me a pellet gun and one of the kids in town named Josh, not my friend Josh from the previous chapter, had said that I shot him in the eye with my pellet gun. His parents called the police. Again I was made to see the District Justice who charged me with harassment even though, one Josh's eye was completely fine, and two my dad told the District Justice that he had taken my pellet gun away from me the week prior for misbehaving with it. I tried telling the officer who came to my house the same thing and woke my dad up to back me up on that which he did. The officer didn't care obviously and neither did the District Justice when I went to see her because she gave me a fine and community service to complete.

The District Justice had also informed me that I had to get a job to pay my fine and she was aware my mom had paid my last fine completely and told me that if my mother would bail me out all the time, I'd never learn my lesson. So my mom was the third shift supervisor at a McDonald's so I had asked her boss if I could have a job and he told me if I work anything like my mom he'd be more then happy to give me a job. So I began working there to pay my fine as well as doing community service at the school. Little did my boss at McDonald's know I don't listen very well. So I'd be loud and obnoxious at work to the point I'd clock in at 4:00pm and by 4:15pm I was calling my mom to come pick me up telling her they were sending me home early. My mom began to wonder why I was constantly being "sent home early" so she asked once day at work and my managers would tell her, "He's loud and he doesn't listen, so we send him home."

My mom was not very happy to hear that and she told me that the next time I "got sent home early" that I'd have to walk home from work because she'd refuse to come get me. Now the thing about work was it was about thirty minutes from my house driving. So when I'd call my mom to pick me up she'd literally just pulled in the driveway from dropping me off at work. Also a thirty minute drive is a LONG walk, especially for a 16 year old. I eventually got better at listening and not being so loud and ended up continuing to work there even after paying off my fine. I worked there for three or four years before I'd eventually voluntarily leave for a better job.

About a year later when I was 17 years old I'd find myself in more trouble with the law. I was hanging out with another kid in town by the name of Ryan. Ryan was another kid I use to smoke cigarettes with. One day we were hanging out and walking through the lumber yard beside my house. Ryan told me he really had to go number two and couldn't wait, So I began walking away. As I walked away I said, "You know poo is flammable right?"

Ryan said, "Yeah right dude, You're lying!" As I continued to walk away I found a pack of matches on the ground. That's all the inspiration I needed to prove what I told Ryan to be true. I took the matches back to Ryan who had done his business in the middle of two building of the lumber yard and we lit his poo on fire. Little did we know the cleaning lady was inside the lumber store and saw us. She called the owner who came by and forced us to stand at his truck until the police came.

Once the police showed up the owner had told the police what we did and showed the police the evidence and the police took Ryan and myself to the police station. We were literally right next to my house and the police took us 3 miles away to the police station and called our parents. My dad came to pick me up and I wished he had not. When I tell you my dad was HEATED, I can't begin to explain just how made he was. I got in his car and when I got home I got the butt whooping of a lifetime. He couldn't believe he had to drive 3 miles to pick me up after I got arrested not even 25 feet from the house.

Once again I had to see the District Justice who by this time was sick and tired of dealing with me. She charged me with arson and gave me a fine to pay and then told me that if she saw me again before I was 18 years old she'd throw me into Juvenile Hall until my 18th birthday and then on my 18th birthday would meet with me again to decided weather or not to let me out or send me to jail. This was the wake up call I needed as I didn't want to go to Juvenile Hall and certainly didn't want to go to jail. Or so I thought it was the wake up call I needed. Because little did I know that wouldn't be the last time I'd find myself in trouble with the law.

Not even a year later when I turned 18 years old I was at work. At this time I worked at a grocery store in the kitchen cooking and prepping food. Jared had called me to hang out and I told him I was at work until 8pm. He told me he'd pick me up from work so I called my ride home and told them I didn't need them to pick me up. At the end of my shift Jared came to pick me up and he had my brother and our friend Chris along. I was super excited because the four of us just spelled trouble but was always fun times.

I got in the car and we drove off. Shortly after that Jared pulled out a BB Gun and began shooting the windows out of cars parked along the side of the road. Chris and my brother began laughing so I laughed as well. Little did I know they had been doing this for the past 23 hours. We drove around shooting car windows out for parked cars for the next 3 hours. We entered a development behind a local elementary school where a cop was sitting in the empty parking lot of the school.

Jared had his headlights off so a few seconds later we saw the blue and red lights flashing behind us. Jared pulled up and when the officer realized who he had just pulled over he called for back up. About three or four more cop cars showed up each with two officers inside them. All the officers drew their guns and ordered us to put our hands above our heads inside the car. Jared at this time had a Toyota Celica so me being a 6 foot 3 inch 18 year old put my hands up against the ceiling the best I could. And officer came a opened Jared's car door and ripped him out of the car and threw him on the ground and ordered him not to move.

My brother, who remember has Cerebral Palsy, freaked out and opened the car door to get out. An office ran up and slammed the door shut before ordering my brother out of the car and detaining him. Next it was my turn, The officer ordered me out of the car so with my hands still up the best I could I began to get out of the car. My foot got stuck in the passenger side seat belt and the officer ripped me out of the car, slapped hand cuffs on me and sat me down in the middle of a giant pile of snow. After we all were out of the car we were all placed into separate police cars and taken to the police station. The remaining officers stayed on the scene to search Jared's vehicle for weapons.

We got to the police station and we were all placed into separate rooms. The police began their investigation by interviewing us all one by one. Little did they know we agreed in the car once we got pulled over that we wouldn't talk no matter what and if we did we wouldn't rat each other out. After the police had basically gotten nowhere with us Jared was taken to the county jail and the rest of us were free to go with the understanding we were to appear before the District Justice. Now remember I'm 3 months into being 18 years old and the last time I saw the District Justice was not even a year ago when she told me if she saw me again before I was 18 years old she put me in Juvi until I was 18 years old and then possibly put me in Jail. So I was pretty sure I was going to jail when she'd see me this time.

I appeared before the District Justice facing 8 counts of Criminal Mischief. I told her my side of the story under a guilty plea and to my surprise she told me that she was dropping all my charges due to a lack of evidence. My brother and Chris weren't so lucky, They were given a fine and community service. As far as Jared he was sentenced to serve time in County Jail. Jared served his time and I would write letters to him quite frequently. After serving enough time to get out on good behavior Jared was released and put on probation which he also completed.

During this time of getting in trouble with the law when I was 15 years old I'd rededicate my life to the Lord at Snow Camp that I talked about in the previous chapter. I decided to rededicate my life to the Lord because I felt like as a kid when I gave my heart of the Lord I didn't quite fully understand what I was doing or what it meant. I wanted to give my heart to the Lord knowing exactly what I was doing and why I was doing it, not because I knew it was the right thing to do. But as you can tell from what you just read about how I got in trouble with the law it really didn't do me much good.

When I was a Senior in high school I attended the Career And Technology Center in Brownstown, Pennsylvania for Graphic's And Printing Technology. This kid from Pequea Valley High School would pick on me everyday. I eventually had enough of it and I told him, "If you don't stop, I'm gonna kill you." The teacher sent me to the principles office and she gave me three days of out of school suspension. This would be the first time I have ever been suspended from school but it also wouldn't be the last. I served my three day suspension and came back to school.

The same kid began picking on me again so I went to my desk, sat down and told the girl I sat next to, "If that kid ever dies, I'm gonna have a party." The teacher again sent me to the principles office where not only the principle was waiting for me but a local police officer as well. The principle told me that the original punishment for a second time offense like this was ten days of out of school suspension and that I'd leave immediately with the police officer who would arrest me on charges of terrorist threats or that since she had talked to the class and quite a few kids told her the kid had been picking on me that she would cut me a deal for three more days of out of school suspension and when I returned I'd be required to spend the rest of the school year doing anger management classes through the school. Of course I took the three days of out of school suspension with completing anger management classes for the rest of the year upon my return since that deal didn't require me to be arrested. So in one week I spent a total of 6 days suspended from school over two different offenses. Because this happened about a month prior to graduation it almost cost me my opportunity to graduate as being out of school for 6 days put me very behind in my school work.

I came back to school after serving the second round of three days of out of school suspension and I had to check in every day with one of the guidance counselor upon my arrival to the school. Then for the first hour of school I had to go to the conference room where the school held it's anger management classes. They taught us about Fight, Flight and Freeze and other ways to manage our anger. My favorite part was that we also got cookies and iced tea so while all my classmates spent their time in class the first hour of school I got to eat cookies and drink iced tea. After the class was over I'd go to my normal class and then before I left for the day I had to check in with the guidance counselor once again. Definitely beat sitting in jail for terrorist threats right?

I started taking online college courses through The International Academy Of Design And Technology, IADT for short, for Graphic Design after I graduated high school in 2009. My parents made it very clear that after I turned 18 years old and graduated high school that I was expected to do one of three things, Go to college, Move out, or Start paying them rent. I chose what in my eyes was the smartest decision and that was going to college.

Now sure I was doing college online so I wasn't actually going away to college but they still gave me the going to college deal. Online college wasn't that bad but it wasn't that enjoyable either. I actually found a way to get in trouble doing online college believe it or not.

Now your probably wondering, "How do you get in trouble going to college online?" Well I'll tell you, We had this drop box we had to turn our assignments and homework and what not into on the portal of the website. You could see everyone who submitted their assignments and you could see their assignment as well. I forgot to do my assignment so I decided to take someone else assignment that was already turned in, copy it, change a few things, and submit it as my own. I got away with this for a little bit but eventually the professor caught on and rightfully accused me of plagiarism. Though the professor was right, Of course I denied it.

The professor took it to the dean of the school and next thing I know I had to meet with the dean of the school regarding my plagiarism of other students assignments. Knowing I was caught and that the jig was up, I confessed to the plagiarism and the dean of the school told me I would be given an F for those assignments even though I turned them in on time and that if I got caught plagiarizing any more assignments that I would be kicked out of the college. This wasn't the only time I'd get in trouble as shortly before I transferred to The Art Institute Of York – Pennsylvania I decided it'd be a good idea to lash out at a teacher and tell her that she was fat and lazy and, well lets say to keep it nice, a female dog. So yeah even in online college I'd find ways to get into trouble.

When I transferred to The Art Institute Of York – Pennsylvania in 2010 I got in trouble again for plagiarism and had to meet with my professor and the dean of that school as well. The professor I had for this class was pretty cool, He'd call me Mtn Dew because I'd come to class everyday with a bottle of Mtn Dew. So because I liked the professor of the class I saved him the trouble and confessed that yes I did copy another study's homework. Just like the time in online college I received and F for the homework and the dean told me that they were aware I had done this before at a previous college so they were taking it a bit more serious then a first time offense and that if I did it again I'd be kicked out of the college. I told them I understood and I never plagiarized an assignment or a homework ever again. I think for once in my life I actually learned a lesson.

<u>*Chapter 4*</u>

DRUGS AND ALCOHOL

*"Do you not know that your bodies are temples
of the Holy Spirit, who is in you, whom you have
received from God? You are not your own; you were
bought at a price. Therefore honor God with your bodies."*
- 1 Corinthians 6:19-20

Remember when I mentioned about my friend Josh and how we both enjoyed watching professional wrestling? Well when I was a teenager that's when CM Punk hit the scene in WWE. And he was all about being "straight edge" he even had this catchphrase, "I'm straight edge, And straight edge means I'm better then you!" I use to tell people as a teenager I don't do drugs because I'm straight edge and that means I'm better then you. The truth was I didn't do drugs because I wasn't old enough to do drugs. I mean sure I smoked cigarettes when I was 15 years old but that didn't last long cause once my mom found out about it, She put a stop to that real quick.

Now that I was 18 years old and old enough to buy a pack a cigarettes that's exactly what I did. I knew nothing about cigarettes like the difference between hundreds or regular sized because when I smoked cigarettes as a teenager it was also pre smoked cigarettes that I was basically just sucking the tar and chemicals out of because there was little to no tobacco left in the cigarettes thus the reason whoever was smoking it put it out. So my dad always smoked Marlboro reds so I went with that because if dad smoked it all those years. They must be good or why would he have smoked them for so long. I really didn't smoke cigarettes that long, a few months maybe because they were just so expensive and I really couldn't afford to pay for the habit so I decided to quite before it became a habit.

After that I began smoking Marijuana. And the story about how I began smoking that is literally quite pathetic. I was hanging out with Jared and we went to a party at this girls house that Jared knew from when he was in school. Chris and his girlfriend at the time, later his wife, now his ex wife, were there to as well as a girl Jared and I knew from youth group and her boyfriend. Everyone began smoking weed out of a bong, passing it around the room. The bong got to me and of course I said, "Nah, I'm good."

The girl who's party it was, Sasha was her name, She stood up came over in front of me, stood in front of me with the bong and said, "You're really gonna sit there and say no to an hot emo girl in a mini skirt?" I said, "Alright" and I took the bong and took a hit. Now the funny part about this was that Sasha wasn't even old enough to smoke cigarettes, So how she got weed is beyond me. That night I can't lie was really fun. Not because of the weed but for a few reason.

At one point Jared passed out and I don't know how this came about or where It came from but we all started yelling, "DIDJA" and Jared would get so pissed because he was trying to sleep and everyone keep yelling, "DIDJA!" Now I still to this day have no idea what didja means or if it even is a word but now it's like an inside joke with Jared cause he still can't to this day stand to hear it. Another point in the night we all were talking and then next thing we knew the girls just started kissing each other and of course us guys being guys were just like,

"AWESOME!" This wouldn't be the last time I smoked weed though. When I went off to college at The Art Institute Of York – Pennsylvania in 2010 lets just say I became really popular on campus after I turned 21 years old in 2011. That's when I started drinking alcohol and magically began to make friends with people on campus who wanted me to buy them alcohol.

My 21st birthday was October 24th, 2011 and my dad picked me up from college and told me we were going to the bar. We went to The Station At The Reinholds Inn which was a bar that was right behind the house I grew up at in Reinholds, Pennsylvania. We walked in and the girl behind the bar was a girl I went to school with who was in my brothers grade. She asked for my I.D and I gave it to her. She saw it was my birthday and said, "What can I get you?" I said, "I don't know, Just give me a Mtn Dew."

She looked at me and said, "It's your 21st birthday, I will not give you a Mtn Dew." I told her how I've never drank before so I don't know what to get. She said, "Well what do you like to drink?" I said, "I like iced tea?" And she started telling me about here there is an alcoholic version of iced tea called a Long Island Iced Tea. I said, "Sure, Let me get one of those!"

She then told me, "We don't have Long Island Iced Tea's here but we do have Twisted Tea which is like a Long Island Iced Tea just a bit weaker when it comes to alcohol content." I had no idea what she was talking about, alcohol content, so I said, "Yeah, That's fine!" So she gave me a Twisted Tea, Wished me a Happy Birthday, and told me the first one was on the house. That bar is historical so it closes around midnight and by that time I had about three Twisted Tea's. We left that bar and went to The Denver House next in Denver, Pennsylvania. Again I was asked for my I.D and I gladly gave it to the girl behind the bar.

She looked at my I.D gave it back to me and said, "Happy Birthday, First ones on me, What can I get you?" This time I didn't say Mtn Dew because I knew something I liked, So I said, "Let me get a Twisted Tea!" The girl said, "We don't have those but we do have Long Island Iced Tea" so I said alright, "Let me get one of those!" That bar closed around one in the morning and I had four Long Island Iced Teas, so my dad took me to another bar. This time it was The Cocalico Tavern in Stevens, Pennsylvania. Again I presented my I.D got my first drink for free.

This bar closed at about two in the morning so I had about two more Twisted Teas. So about 4 Long Island Iced Teas and 5 Twisted Teas as the final count for the night among the three bars we went to, my dad and I left the Cocalico Tavern. I got out in the parking lot stumbling and fumbling and said to my dad, "Which ones your car?" He said, "You know which one my car is, It's the white Subaru." I said, "I know, But there's three white Subaru's parked next to each other!" He said, "Man, You're TRASHED!"

He took me back to my moms house in Reinholds as my mom and dad didn't live together anymore at this point, We will get into that later in this book though. I went up the steps and passed out in the living room. My mom woke up the next morning and said, "Your dad got you drunk didn't he!" My head was pounding and every word she spoke rang through my head like a gong. My mom eventually took me back to college and now it was time to party at college cause I was 21 years old and old enough to drink, which meant I was old enough to party the right way!

I began buying my roommates in college alcohol, They'd give me the money, I'd hop on my bike and go to the alcohol store, come back and give them their alcohol. Soon more and more kids on campus had me running for alcohol for them or their parties and what not. So I'd start getting invited to all these parties on campus as I was the reason they actually had alcohol so of course I was invited. At a majority of these parties we would not only drink alcohol but we would also smoke weed. It also helped that I was roommates with both members of CoferCop who were also two fourths of 4Ceen. CoferCop was my roommates Jonathan and Khiary's rap duo name and 4Ceen was the name of a group of rappers on campus consisting of my two roommates Jonathan and Khiary, and their friends Ashley aka King+1 and J.R. We'd often go to the recording studio at college, They'd drop a few bars and beats, then we'd come and we'd smoke weed till sometimes two or three in the morning.

I remember one time we were drinking and smoking and I got so drunk, I drank an entire bottle of Mad Dog 20/20 aka MD 20/20 and I couldn't even stand up straight. Jonathan, Khiary, and our other roommate Darrell had to literally carry me home and put me to bed. We got halfway home and the campus Security guard was out and they guys were like, "Dude, Jaime you gotta look cool or your gonna get in trouble." So I tried my hardest to look sober and act sober. I'm pretty sure we just sat on the curb until he went by acting like we were just sitting there talking like friends. Looking back on it now that was quite embarrassing to have 3 guys younger then me have to legit carry me home and tuck my grown self in.

Another time I was really high we were going to Ashley's house I think it was, cause he lived off campus, And we were in the car listening to their music they made and I'm in the back seat with Khiary and I just yelled, TEAM DIRTY!" Now Team Dirty was the name the guys used to refer to their fans so this was really hilarious. They turned off the music and had me say it again, so I yelled, "TEAM DIRTY!" Little did I know they had recorded me and then when they're next set of music came out, in the beginning of the one track you can here me yell, "TEAM DIRTY!" I can't lie it's kind of cool to know I'm on one of their tracks even if it is for point zero three milliseconds.

Another story I have from partying at college is the night I spent drinking and watching March Madness at my friend David's condo with our friend Kelsi and Maggie. We were drinking Four Loko's and Kelsi was getting so mad that the team she was rooting for wasn't doing good that she began smacking the television screen. I was like, "Kelsi you do know they can't feel you hitting them right?" She was like, "Shut up I know that!" Kelsi was a little firecracker when she was mad, She was about 5 foot nothing but boy she could hold her own.

Kelsi screaming at the television.

I believe it was that same night Maggie got so drunk that Kelsi and I had to walk her home. We walked her to her condo, I opened the front door as wide as I could and said, "Ok, Now all you have to do is walk in the door." She started walking into her condo and then, BAM, She walked right into the bricks of the condo. We helped her get inside and then left. The next morning she came to class with a black eye and her nose was massive.

After my time in college I came home and I began hanging out with this guy who was my sisters age, his name was Adam, and his friend Christian. I'd pick them up and drive them to Lancaster, Pennsylvania where they'd go into this house and come back out. I never asked any questions until we go back to Christians house and went in his back yard. Adam pulled out what looked like the brownest Marijuana I've ever seen. I said, "What is that?" He said, It's Spice, You know K2, Synthetic Marijuana." I said, "Oh Ok, So it's like Marijuana, Cool!"

We began smoking it, They rolled it like a cigarette. I know now that it was not like Marijuana. This stuff got me so high I could barely function. I began starring off into space and at one point was starring at Adam, he said, "Dude, Why you starring at my balls" I said, "I'm not, Your balls are starring at me!" Now that makes absolutely no sense what so ever but I was so high I couldn't even think about what I was saying. This was around the time that K2 first hit the scene so the police didn't even know much about it let alone what it was.

I only hung out with Adam and Christian for a few months after coming home from college because one day I supposed to pick up Adam take him to Lancaster and then he wanted to go to Reading, Pennsylvania to pick up his friend Ashley. Adam was cool so I assumed Ashley was to. Now this next part I haven't told many people about for fear of being judged like I was when I got into trouble with Jared and had my charges dropped then. The day I was supposed to pick up Adam and take him to pick up Ashley I got called into work. I was working at the grocery store in the kitchen that I mentioned previously in this book when I talked about getting into trouble with Jared. I told my boss I'd be in and I told Adam I couldn't pick him up.

Thankfully work saved my butt that day because Adam got his friend Ryan to pick him up and take him to get Ashley. Ryan and Adam picked up Ashley took her to Middle Creek and because Ashley wouldn't have sex with Adam, They stabbed her and left her for dead in the Projects. Stupidly they came back the next day to burn her body to make sure she was indeed dead and they were arrested for the murder of Ashley. Ryan and Adam were sentenced to Life In Prison and the state I believe it was had pushed for them to receive the death penalty but the judge found that unconstitutional and sentenced them to Life In Prison. So had I not been called into work that day or had I told my boss I could, I may be sitting in a prison cell right now charged with murder or something like that instead of writing this book. After that day I never touched Marijuana or K2 ever again!

Around the time that I turned 29 years old I started chewing tobacco. I began getting Skoal Wintergreen pouches and later switched to Copenhagen Southern Blend Long Cut. Jared also chewed tobacco so when we hung out we were always chewing tobacco. I couldn't afford a mud jug so I made my own spit container using an empty Johnny Bootlegger glass bottle. I wrapped it in copper brown duct tape and then put a We The People sticker on it and then wrapped it in packaging tape. That thing was indestructible, I dropped it quite a few times and it didn't break. It truly was a nasty habit.

I remember a few times I had a drink and I always had my spit bottle near by me wherever I was. Id go to grab my drink and not paying attention I'd grab my spit bottle. Usually I'd realize it before I got the bottle to my mouth but there was a couple times I didn't realize until it was to late and I had a mixture of old chewing tobacco and spit enter in my mouth. Another thing that use to happen not to often but more then I'd liked it to was I'd spill my spit bottle and that was a mess. I even use to chew tobacco while sitting in church. I'd never have my spit bottle with me though I'd just stomach it.

I usually went through about one sleeve which is 5 cans in two weeks. Whenever I'd get paid from work I'd go to the convenience store next to my house and I'd buy 1 sleeve of Copenhagen Southern Blend Long Cut, although for a while it seemed like they never had it in stock. I was quite annoying as then I'd have to go elsewhere to get my tobacco and I'd have to have someone drive me. People found my habit of chewing tobacco to be disgusting and rightfully so because when someone is constantly spitting in a bottle or on the ground around you it's kind of like, "Dude, Can you stop?" I'd even go to family functions like Christmas or Thanksgiving and I had to find a cup that I could spit into and then I'd leave it sit and go outside or something and family member would find it and be like, "Are you serious Jaime, Don't leave your nasty cups of spit laying around." It really was a nasty habit that made people very uncomfortable.

At the time I began chewing tobacco I worked at a Nursing Home And Rehabilitation Center as a Dietary Cook. And yes I'm sure you guessed it, I would chew tobacco while I would be preparing the food and cooking the food that I'd later serve to the residents of the facility. I'd have the trash can next to were I was working and I'd spit into the trash can as I was preparing and or cooking food. Looking back on that now it was as disgusting as I thought it was when I saw another Dietary Cook there who also chewed tobacco spitting his tobacco into the trash can as he prepared and cooked food. I'd eventually leave that job but come back 5 months later after the job I left for didn't work out and I would be rehired as a Housekeeper. This was when COVID became a big thing and you had to wear a mask everywhere you went.

I loved having to wear a mask at work because guess what, I would have a wad of chewing tobacco in my mouth as I'd go room to room in the facility cleaning the residents rooms. I'd look around and make sure nobody was looking and I'd spit into the trash can on my Housekeeping cart then I'd put my mask back up. To be honest, I don't think I have everybody fooled as I'm pretty sure there was a few people there who knew but I did think I was pretty slick for this. The good thing was I have a pretty good gag reflex so I was able after a while to even "stomach it" so that nobody for sure could tell I had chewing tobacco in my mouth. But I had my can of chewing tobacco in my back pocket at all times so that stuck out like a sore thumb. I'm pretty sure a few people residents included had asked me if I chew tobacco seeing the round imprint in the back of my pants I wear for work where I kept my can of chewing tobacco.

The only remotely semi cool story I have about chewing tobacco is that one year around Christmas time I started saving all my empty chewing tobacco cans. I'm pretty sure I ever asked Jared if I could have his and he thought that was weird that I wanted his empty chewing tobacco cans, which I don't blame him. I stacked them on a table in my living room kind of like you see a display stacked in the store. I had to of had like thirty or forty empty chewing tobacco cans stacked together. Jared came over one day and I told him, "Do you like my Dipmas tree." He was like, "You really made a Christmas tree out of empty chewing tobacco cans?"

I even took a picture of it and put it on Instagram. What can I say, I'm a creative person. This was the most creative thing I've ever thought of. The only thing that was somewhat annoying was if someone would accidentally knock it over because then the cans would go everywhere and I had to re-stack them and it was just a pain in the butt. But come on you got to admit Dipmas instead of Christmas, That's pretty good right?

Chapter 5

CAUGHT IN THE MIDDLE

"Love is patient, Love is kind. It doesn't envy,
It doesn't boast, it is not proud. It doesn't dishonor
others, it is no self-seeking, it is not easily
angered, and it keeps no record of wrongs."
- 1 Corinthians 13:4-7

When I was 17 years old my parents separated after 18 years of marriage. Now before I dive to far into this topic I just want to say I love my mom and my dad both. I have absolutely no ill feelings towards either of them for their separation and later divorce. I don't know if the fact I was a junior in high school had anything to do with my feelings toward them no longer being together. But all I know is it happened, I got threw it and life goes on. All I'll say is that I knew my parents would argue, but I never thought it was that bad to were it would destroy our family.

When it happened I was pretty tore up. And the reason I was tore up over it was because I always told myself, "Sure mom and dad argue but they'll never get divorced. They argue just like any other couple, It isn't so serious that they'll get a divorce." So when it did happen I was like, "Well damn, That isn't what I expected. I remember the night my dad had to leave, My sister and I got his things and brought them out to him cause he wasn't allowed on the property of the house. After all his stuff was out of the house he went to live with one of his friends in Denver, Pennsylvania.

I was 17 years old and my sister was 15 years old. My parents decided to settle things out of court as far as my dad paying to support us. My sister and I continued to live with our mom. My mom never once kept us from seeing our dad and even encouraged us to continue having a healthy relationship with our dad despite them no longer being together. My dad took things hard, He would randomly buy us stuff or try to do things to, in what I believe was to, "prove his love to us" but little did he know he didn't have to prove anything to us as my sister and I knew he still loved us and that separation wasn't what he wanted. I remember one time my brother and I were over at where my dad lived and I was telling my dad how KISS was coming to Hershey, Pennsylvania. KISS is my dads favorite band and played it all the time when I was a kid so it became my favorite band as well.

Next thing I know my dad is on his cellphone with a representative from Ticketmaster ordering three tickets to see KISS "The Hottest Show On Earth" in Hershey, Pennsylvania. Now when I told him about this show I had absolutely zero expectations of him actually buying tickets to go, In fact I never even asked him to or remotely poked the idea of him doing so. We went to the concert when it came around and we had a blast. We had seats in the bleachers of the Hershey Stadium and the show was so empty the

Me and Gene Simmons, possibly a person dressed up like Gene Simmons at The Hottest Show On Earth Tour October 2010 in Hershey, PA

security guards started coming up the bleachers telling people in the bleachers they could move down to the floor section so long as they didn't try to get into the VIP section. We went down to the floor section and ended up being so close that when KISS took the stage and set of pyro we could feel the heat from the pyro heating up our skin. Before the show though my brother and I went for a walk around the stadium.

We saw a crowd of people on the left hand side of the stage and a ton of security surrounding the area, so we went to investigate. Here it was Gene Simmons meeting with fans, We were shocked. We stood in line and eventually got our picture taken with Gene Simmons. Now when I tell everyone this they all say, "Yeah right how do you know it was actually Gene Simmons, People go to those concerts dressed up like the band members all the time." And I say, " Oh Yeah, Well would a big bad buff biker dude take a picture of his wife with a fake Gene Simmons as the fake Gene Simmons stares directly at his wife's boobs and not beat the crap out of the fake Gene Simmons?" Also, "why would there have been like literally eight to ten security guards all around a fake Gene Simmons?"

My brother and I were so excited that we ran back to my dad and said, "Dad, Dad, We saw Gene Simmons, And we got our picture with him!" The opening band was a band called Envy they were alright, Not really my cup of tea though. KISS was all we cared about though. At one point the part of the stage that Paul Stanley was one lifted up and came out over the crowd. He stopped right about the section where my dad, my brother, and I were standing. Paul Stanley was maybe ten to fifteen feet about our heads.

Another time I went to visit my dad, I remember he offered me weed and beer. I was old enough for the weed but not for the beer. I declined both as this was still during my, "I'm straight edge and straight edge means I'm better then you" phase. It honestly wasn't until my parents separated and I didn't get to see my dad 24/7/365 that I really understood what he meant when he said to me as a kid when he had to discipline me, "someday you'll understand I do this out of love and not because I enjoy it." My dad use to discipline me as a kid and I'd tell him, "I HATE you!" After my parents separated is when I really began to regret ever saying that to my dad because we'd begin to become closer through this time.

Dad dated after the separation but didn't really find a solid relationship until after he and my mom officially divorced two years later. My mom on the other hand she had found a boyfriend pretty quick and of course he moved in pretty quick as well. Her boyfriends name was John and in the beginning he was alright. My mom worked third shift at a new by convenience store so John and I would go to the store when she was working and hang out for hours. One time after I finally got my drivers license John and I went to Saturdays Market in Middletown, Pennsylvania to a toy store where WWE Superstar and at that time WWE Champion Kane was going to be making an appearance. I got my picture taken with Kane and it was the coolest thing ever.

John let me drive his Ford Torus and once we hit the highway John told me, "Open it up." I was like, "What" he said, "Gun it!" So I put the peddle to the metal and we hit 120 miles per hour. One night my mom let me use her Ford Aerostar to hang out with some friends on the understanding that I be at her work before

WWE Superstar Kane and I at Saturdays Market in Middletown, PA in 2012

6:00am to pick her up from work. So the next day I went to pick her up and John came with. I don't know what happened but he just went crazy telling me, " Go this way, Go that way, Turn here, Turn there!" Then next thing I knew he's on the phone with 911 telling them that he's Jesus and people are following us and coming from out of state to get him.

He made me drive to his brothers house who wasn't very happy that we showed up randomly so early in the morning. His brother told him to get the eff off his property and told me to drive home and not listen to John. I was crying because I knew my mom was going to be pissed that she had to walk home from work since I wasn't there to pick her up and John's brother told me, "Don't worry about it, I'll call your mom and let her know what happened and that you're on your way home." I got home and John's brother had indeed called my mom and filled her in on what happened. My mom was pissed at John instead of me. I was never cool with John ever again as for 2 hours this man hand me driving around like a maniac because he was psychotic, He basically kidnapped me as if I refused to do what he said he'd say to me, "Who's side are you on mine or there?" I had no idea who "there's" was and to this day I still have no idea.

This between John and I really went down hill from there. Just like Tyler when I was a kid, I'd tell John, "You're not my dad, I don't have to listen to you." One time John and I were arguing and he grabbed me by my shirt collar and pinned me against the kitchen sink. Jared was over and saw this so he leaped over the dinning room table and punched John right in his jaw. Needless to say I wasn't allowed to have friends over after that. Quite a few times our arguments would result in my putting John in a headlock and dragging him to the stairs with the intent on tossing his down the stairs and out the door.

The only thing that stopped me was my mom

screaming, "Stop, I love him!" Once I heard my mom screaming in her bedroom so I ran in to see why she was screaming and saw John throwing books at my mom. I put him in a headlock, threw him over my should onto the bed and said, "You don't throw s**t at my mom, Or any women for that matter, You hear me?!" He eventually did it again so I went into the room to see him again throwing stuff at my mom but this time he was completely naked. I knew I had to either let him get away with it or deal with him while he was completely naked. I chose the second option, I put him in a headlock, threw him on the bed and said, "What did I tell you about throwing stuff at my mom!"

John would then want to make me pay more rent and it would make me pay more then my mom and John were paying so I refused. John and I got into and argument over it and I eventually said to my mom, "This guy doesn't love you, I DO, You need to chose, Is it gonna be me or him!" She said, "I can't leave him, I have nowhere to go." I said, "Fine, Then I'm looking for my own place and moving out as soon as possible." I called my uncle and asked if I could move in with him until I found my own place and he said yes. So I packed my things and moved in with my uncle in Ephrata, Pennsylvania.

I lived with my uncle for three or four month before I got a room above the Denver House in Denver, Pennsylvania. It was a twelve foot by fifteen foot room on the third floor, the guy next to me was a schizophrenic and the bathroom was shared between like ten rooms. I was paying three hundred and fifty dollars a month to live there. And boy do I have memories from living there. There were the late night's at the bar downstairs. And can't forget the landlord wife coming up the steps from the bar cracking her taser yelling, "I don't wanna hear nothing from no one tonight or you'll be sorry!"

Jared was over one night and he went to sit on the floor and he misjudged amount of space left between his butt and the floor and fell back against the wall. Of all the walls to fall against it had to be the wall separating my room from the room of the guy who was schizophrenic. They guy comes over to my door and knocks on the door, Now the landlord told me if this ever happened to ignore him and not answer the door. So I told that to Jared but Jared doesn't listen so well, He opened the door and the neighbor guy punches Jared in the face and then gets on top of him and wrestles him on the floor. I got my pellet gun out and pressed it against the neighbors temple and told him, "You can leave with two eyes or you can leave with one, You choice!" By this time the landlord has come down to my room to see what all the commotion was about.

He told me to put my gun away in which I did. The guy across from my room laughed and said, "Put that toy gun away, What are you gonna do with that?" I said, "It may be a toy but if you know how to use it you can cause a good bit of damage so I'd shut up if I were you!" The landlord ordered the schizophrenic neighbor back to his room and apologized to me. Jared and I had a good laugh over that.

Then there was the time Jared came over and we were drinking in my room. He told me he had to go to the bathroom so he left my room and went down to the bathroom. After quite some time of him not coming back I went to check on him, I knocked on the bathroom door and I asked him if he was alright. He said he was alright and then I heard glass shatter. I said, "What was that" as he opened the bathroom door and ran down the hallway out the door and into his car and sped off. In the bathroom the mirror above the sink was broken and glass was all over the floor.

The landlord was pissed and rightfully so. I called

Jared and said, "What the hell man?" He said, "I saw someone in the mirror and freaked out" I said, "Yeah, that was YOU in the mirror ya idiot." The landlord told me Jared was no longer allowed on the property until he either paid for a new mirror or provided the landlord with a new mirror to replace the one he broke. Jared was really good at causing trouble if you couldn't already tell.

In January of 2015 a family acquaintance of twenty plus years who worked with my mom and grandma at the convenience store offered to let me move in with him. He lived in the next building down from the Denver House. He told me since he works third shift he never really comes out of his room other then to use the bathroom, shower, and to eat and that I'd have the entire house to myself because of that. He sweetened the deal by telling me he'd charge me the same as I was paying to live at the Denver House only where he lives I'd have more room. So I took him up on his offer and moved in. I had a friend who owned a tow truck business at the time and I loaded all my belongings on the back on his flat bed and I even got to sit on the back of his flat bed tow truck to make sure nothing feel off in the maybe fifty foot trip from the Denver House to where I was moving to.

I got settled into the new place with the family acquaintance, his name was Paul." I called my mom and I told her that if she left John, as she was still living with John, she could keep her things at my place until she found a place. She told me, "I have nowhere to go." Eventually about two years later she called me and asked if the deal I made her was still good. I asked her, "Are you going to leave John?" She said, "Yes", I told her, "Then bring your stuff you have no room for over."

She bought over a few boxes of things and I put then in the storage under my steps. I was so glad she finally saw the light and left that bum. She was physically unhealthy and mentally unhealthy due to his manipulation though she would never admit he was manipulative towards her. But I didn't care all I cared about was that she was no longer with him. She even got a no contact order against him and I had her add my name and info to it as well so John couldn't contact me either. Although he contacted my mom and I on numerous occasions after that and even professed his love for me and how he wished I would open my eyes to new things when I told him I wasn't gay and had no interest in being gay.

A year or two after moving into the apartment with Paul, Jared had gotten released from county jail for a probation violation and needed a place to stay to avoid going back to jail. I had convinced Paul to let Jared move in with us. Jared moved in which was great because now I didn't have to call or text my best friend to hang out because he was living under the same roof as me. Living together was so much fun. Chris would come over all the time and at this time he was dating the girl he dated before his wife. Jared, Chris, and I had a party at the house one time and Chris' girlfriend and her friend Jess were over. Now Chris' girlfriend Sierra and Jess weren't old enough to drink, but were drinking, Sierra's dad is a police officer with the local police department.

My neighbor absolutely HATES me and calls the police on me every chance she gets. She called the police and filed a noise complaint so two officers showed up at the apartment, one of which was Sierra's dad. Sierra knew her dad would show up when we saw the flashing lights outside the apartment so her and Jess ran upstairs and hid under my bed. The officer who wasn't Sierra's dad asked if they could come in and I said, "Do you have a warrant?" He said, "No" I said, "Then you can't come in" He said "We're here on a noise complaint" I said, "Alright, We'll turn it down." Sierra's dad said, "Is my daughter here" I said, "Maybe" he said, "I see her car here I wanna talk to my daughter, I'm not asking a a police officer I'm asking as her father" I said, "Well then you can get off my property because no one invited you here so your technically trespassing and if you don't leave I'll have you buddy here escort you off my property."

He looked at his partner and his partner said, "You did kind of just denounce yourself as a police officer so, Yeah your gonna have to go back to the cruiser." Her dad stormed back to the cruised pissed as ever. I yelled inside for someone to turn the music down and they did so the other officer Thank me and went on his way. I went upstairs and told Sierra and Jess that it was safe to come out. Sierra asked if her dad showed up and I said, "Yup" and I told her what happened and she said, "He's gonna be pissed when I get home!" Another time we were having a party and I had to go to work, I worked third shift and Chris told me to call off. So I figured I could call the number I call to clock in and clock in then call again when I was to clock out and clock out and my boss wouldn't know I never went in, My boss knew and he fired me!

After my mom left John she started seeing a new guy. I was happy for her, until I found out who this new guy was. It was my ex girlfriends dad, I was like, "Mom you can't go out with him, I dated his daughter for like a years if not longer." When I broke up with his daughter he looked me dead in my eyes and said, "I never wanna see you again!" And quite frankly I had no intentions of him ever seeing me again. Although I never thought he'd end up dating my mom either.

Things would get even weirder for me when my mom told me she was going to be marrying him. I was like, "Mom, Please don't make me one of those weirdo's who can say they kissed their step sister." Well she went through with marrying him and now I can say I kissed my step sister before she was my step sister and we even dated for at least a year. To be honest though he is a great guy, A lot better then John could ever be. And he makes my mom happy so that's always a plus. He also knows I'll never call him dad or step dad so there's that to.

Going over to their house is pretty awkward though because I have to see my ex girlfriend who still lives there as well as her grandma who lived there when we dated as well because it's technically her house. Now my brother lives there after getting into an altercation with my uncle who also lived at my grandparents house that ended up in my uncle calling the police and my grandparents telling the police they couldn't handle having my brother live there anymore due to conflict with the neighbors. So yeah, Every time I go over to where my mom and her husband live I always feel weird seeing my ex girlfriend who is now my step sister. I don't even think I say hi to her when I go over there. It's just really really weird and awkward to be there so I try to avoid at all costs having to go over there at all.

My Dad also found somebody after he and my mom officially divorced. I told her, "I hope you don't think I'm going to call you mom or step mom because if so you're sadly mistaken." She told me, "I have kids of my own so I don't expect you to call me mom or step mom, even though I do love your dad and I love his kids as well as my own." My dad and his girlfriend ended up having a convenience marriage which from what I understand is where your marriage is recognized by the church but not by the state. Like my moms now husband, the woman my Dad is now with makes him happy so that's all that I care about. She gets bonus points thought because like me she is a Baltimore Ravens fans.

As far as my apartment goes, Paul and Jared have both moved out so I now live in the apartment by myself. It's nice but living in a 4 bedroom, 1 bathroom, upstairs and downstairs apartment by yourself does tend to get lonely at times. The best part of living alone is that I get to make the rules and I get to break the rules and nobody can yell at me as long as I break the rules within the confines of my rental agreement. Jared moved out because he missed living on his own, and Paul well I don't really know what happened to Paul. I woke up one day to find him not home and after his work getting a hold of me concerned cause he didn't show up for work and never called to say he wasn't coming in I checked his bedroom to see if he was in there to find his bedroom completely trashed. After his work filing a missing persons report the police found him and told us that all he wanted us to know is that he is fine, no more, no less.

<u>Chapter 6</u>

SHATTERED DREAMS

*"Rise again, ...for though the righteous fall
seven times, they rise again, but the wicked
stumble when calamity strikes."*
- Proverbs 24:16

Ever since I became really interested in art in middle school I knew I wanted to go to college for something to do with art. As I neared to graduating I began looking into art schools. I originally wanted to go to Pennsylvania College of Art and Design in Lancaster, Pennsylvania and was accepted into the college but later would have my acceptance letter taken back due to the fact they "did realize I had applied for Graphic Design and they don't have a Graphic Design program" even though their website clearly stated they did. They tried telling me the Graphic Design program wasn't yet available. So after that I decided for some reason that I wanted to go to college online so I applied to the International Academy of Design and Technology and was accepted into their Graphic Design program. So in 2009 after I graduated high school I started my classes there.

As I said early in this book I would eventually transfer from IADT to The Art Institute of York – Pennsylvania to their Graphic Design program. I was able to transfer about twenty of my credits knocking out a few classes from the program for AI York. I was able to move into my condo in June or July of 2010 and would start my program in October 2010. I checked into the school when I got there, received my bag of art supplies, and was assigned a condo which were the dorms. They were like townhouses that they had 4 people live in each. Each townhouse had 2 single bedrooms and 1 double bedroom, I had part of the double bedroom and the single bedrooms costed more.

They told me my condo would be condo 3550, so that is where I went. I walked in and my three roommates where already there, I took one look at them and said to my mom, "Oh crap, I'm in trouble." She said, "Why" I told her, "These guys a black, Have you heard how loosely I use the N word?" She said, "You'll be fine" I went in and kept to myself. A few days later the three of them were in one of the single bedrooms playing video games. They all knew each other and where actually friends back home and had planned so they would be housed together.

Jonathan saw me standing in the doorway of the room and said, "Come sit down, You like video games?" I said, " Yeah" and I sat down with them and from that day on we got along great. Khiary had the other single bedroom and Darrell would be sharing the double bedroom with me. They were all from Baltimore, Maryland from the Woodlawn and Milford areas. One night we ended up having a four hour conversation about our religious views. It was the most intelligent and respectful conversation on religion that I've ever had with anyone. We never argued once and we let each other talk about their beliefs and stayed respectful of each others beliefs even if we disagreed with their beliefs.

We all even liked football minus Darrell he wasn't really a fan of sports. Jonathan was a Chicago Bears fan, Khiary was a Cincinnati Bengals fan, and I was a Baltimore Ravens fan, Khiary wasn't to fond of that. I even told them how I wanted to move to Baltimore someday and they all said, "No you don't." I said, "Why not" they said, "Cause in Baltimore all the windows are boarded up in the house that aren't occupied because people break in and do drugs and stuff." We all had a lot in common honestly and rarely ever argued.

Another memory I have from my time in college is the time it snowed, There was a respectable four to six inches on the ground that night. Jonathan, Khiary, Darrell and myself were all in our condo and one of them dared me to run across the parking lot without my shoes or socks on. I agreed to do it so Jonathan opened the door and I ran out into the snow, I got across the parking lot as they were cheering me on and then I got halfway back and they shut the door. I didn't know this at the time but Khiary was filming the entire thing on his Flip digital camera and Darrell got in the frame and said, "And now we go bed." Khiary ended the video with me banging on the door telling them to let me in. After a few good seconds they did end up opening the door and letting me back in. My feet were so cold they were glowing red.

Then this other time I had bought some weed and brought it home. I got into our condo and went up to my room that I shared with Darrell. We had housing inspections the next day which was were the group of students who lived on campus to make sure the rules were being followed and that things on campus didn't get out of hand would come to each condo and look around the house for any damages, rule violations, contraband, etc. The college was also a dry campus which meant absolutely no drugs or alcohol of any kind even if you were of age. Darrell could smell the weed I had that I was in the process of hiding in my sock drawer of my dresser. He said, "Is that weed" I said, "Yeah" He said, "And if you get caught with it tomorrow during house inspections what are you going to tell them?"

I knew this was Darrell's was of hinting at the fact

that I better claim ownership of it if it if it was found during inspections because he knew if I didn't they would kick us both out. So I told him, "I'll tell them it's mine" and he said, "You better because if you don't I'll beat the crap out of you!" I knew Darrell was serious because prior to this I had tried to punch Darrell in a minor dispute we had. He caught my first mid are and threw me over his should onto the floor and said, "Never try to tee me again!" I never did try to hit Darrell again after that day. Housing Inspections came and went and the weed I had hidden in my sock drawer was never found, Thankfully!

As I got to know Darrell, Khiary and Jonathan better I found out that Khiary and Jonathan made rap music together and were a duo called CoferCop, Jonathan's rap name was Cofer aka K9 and Khiary's rap names Cop aka K13 or Koldhearted. I listened to there music and it was really good, So I began going to the studio at the school with them which is how I met Ashley aka King+1 and Josh aka J.R. I'd later come to find out that Jonathan, Khiary, Josh, and Ashley started group known as 4Ceen. As their music became known around campus and they grew more and more popularity on campus our condo, 3550, became one of the primary hang out spots on campus, They even referenced it in their music a few times and eventually it became known as "legendary." So I get to say that I was one fourth of the 3550 Legends! The more I hung out with the guys from 4Ceen the more people I began to become introduced to on campus.

I have to admit after being bullied my enter life and going to college with the expectation of being bullied as well I was pretty weird to have friends and actually have people treat me with respect. The guys from 4Ceen and their little group weren't my only friends on campus though as I previously mentioned David, Kelsi and Maggie back in the chapter where I talked about my drinking alcohol. Kelsi lived in the condo straight across from the condo I stayed in. As I mentioned before she was this little five foot nothing firecracker of a girl. We were such good friends that we'd come over to each other's condo's ring the doorbell and walk right in. Now I had a habit of sleeping until about noon if I didn't have class that morning.

Kelsi would come up to my room stand beside my bed, bend down till she was about an inch from my face and yell, "HEY, WAKE UP!" Scared the crap out of me every time. When she found out I was a fan of Professional Wrestling she told me how her dad was to and how his favorite superstar was John Cena. I wrinkled my nose at that one, She then told me that if her dad ever asked if she had boys in her room at school it was very important that I tell him, NO, and that it was even more important that if he asked if they were boys of color I again tell him, NO! I asked her way and she told me next time her dad came to visit I was to ask him if I could see what was in the back of his truck. So when Kelsi's dad came to visit the next time I asked him if I could see what was in the back of his truck.

He took me to the back of his truck, opened the cab and laying in the back of the truck was none other then a shot gun. I asked him, "Whats that for" he said, "If I find out there are any color boys in my daughters room ever, I will shoot them!" That's all I needed to hear, Kelsi was right her dad was the most racist man I had ever met. Another memory I have of my friendship with Kelsi during college was the time I decided I was going to stop drinking so much Mtn Dew. I would drink about twenty bottles of twenty ouch Mtn Dew's a week. I told Kelsi, "If you see me trying to buy a Mtn Dew, yell at me, and she did. Talk about a good and loyal friend right.

After a few days I began to shake worse and worse with each passing moment. We had determined that I was going through caffeine withdraw which made no sense to me cause I was still drinking soda and caffeinated beverages, Just not Mtn Dew. So I eventually caved and went back to drinking Mtn Dew. Kelsi was from a small town here in Pennsylvania called, Oxford, Maggie was from Reading, Pennsylvania and was a fan of the band Texas In July before they went mainstream which I was to so that's pretty much how we became friend. I even told her about the time I went to see Texas In July before they went mainstream and the lead singer reached down from the stage, grabbed me by my shirt collar, and screamed the lyrics to one of their songs in my face and later threw water on the crowd in the section my sister and I were in. And David he was from Pittsburgh, Pennsylvania and was the biggest Pittsburgh Penguins fan and fan of Sydney Crosby I have ever met. I use to pick on David for being a Penguins fan and liking as I call him "Cry Baby Crosby" but it was all out of good fun and friendship so he never took it personally in fact he use to pick on me for being a Philadelphia Flyer's fan.

Now lets talk about some memories from the actual school itself. I had this professor for this one class who told us that, "Idea's are like a fart, They come quick and some of them stink." Another professor I had he always came to class with a big fat cigar in his mouth. On break he would come outside with us students to the smoking area and smoke his cigar. The odd part was no matter how much he smoked this cigar it somehow remained the same size day after day. Then there was the time that it was Valentines Day and the school would usually have a table with treats on it for each holiday.

Well like I said it was Valentines Day so they decided it would be a good idea to put individually wrapped condoms on the table. Now I don't know who's bright idea it was to put condoms on a table in college setting and encourage kids to take them for FREE. That person just needs to be fired or never allowed to give an idea ever again because, what do you think we the students did with those condoms? We most certainly didn't use them to practice safe intercourse with, No we used them as balloon's. We would sit in class blowing them up and letting the fly down the hallways or across the class room, exactly what you'd expect from college kids. I genuinely have no clue how they expected anything else to happen in a setting like that.

One of the kids at college even had this idea for an after school club called Flow Session. It truly was an interesting concept. There was a good half a dozen of us maybe a few more who ended up attending. There was a giant brown piece of paper, like one from a factory roll of paper covering the tables. We could draw anything we wanted on the paper and since the paper covered the entire table everyone was drawing on the same piece of paper at the same time. So in the end everyone's drawings were on the same paper and made up one giant piece of art.

I even entered the poetry contest one year at college and I ended up placing first if I remember correctly. The topic was the number eleven and our poems had to be seven lines long. Honestly I didn't even really think about my poem or plan it out. I just sat down and typed out seven lines of that first thing that came to mind and submitted it for the poetry contest. If I remember correctly Khiary my roommate his poem got third place. Here is the exact poem that I entered into the poetry contest that ended up getting me first place.

Eleven

"The number Eleven,
reminds me of heaven,
A foot minus an inch,
Overlooked in a sinch,
A perfect example of what friends do,
Sticking together just like glue,
The new one plus one equals Eleven."

I didn't do to bad when it came to my grades in college. I maintained my typical C's and occasional B's despite my staying up all night and partying with the other kids on campus, Getting drunk as a skunk and high as a kit every night. But the one class that gave me the absolute worst trouble was Algebra. Now I've never was very good at mathematics, when I was in grade school after being diagnosed with A.D.D I was put into learning support classes which wasn't exactly your normal classes but wasn't the classes with the kids who ate glue sticks for a snack. So outside of addition, subtraction, multiplication and division we weren't really taught anything else math wise, and if we were we spent the bare minimum that the teacher was required to spend teaching it. Algebra was one of those things we spent the bare minimum learning in learning support so I never really was good at it.

In college we had to complete three levels of mathematics, Basic Math, Elementary Algebra, and College Math. The class you started in was determined by how well you did on the placement test prior to your first semester at the college. I didn't do so hot on that test so I had to start in Basic Math. I failed Basic Math twice and passed it the third and final time I was able to take it, So I spent three semesters trying to pass that class which each semester was three months long so that nine months I spent in Basic Math. Then I went on to Elementary Algebra I failed the class the first time even with the help of a tutor so the next semester I signed up for it again. And once again I failed the class.

The third and final time I took the class I tried so hard, I truly did. I'd be one of the first people all the time to arrive to class and one of if not the last one to leave every time. When we had a test I always took my time and was always one of the last people to turn in my test, I even continued to meet with my tutor as well as stayed after class a few times to get help from the professor herself.

When I knew the final exam was coming up I was excited I had a passing grade for once, sure it was just barely passing but it was a passing grade none the less. So I was determined to let NOTHING pull my grade down. I studied nigh and day, I slept with my notes under my pillow, I had my roommate and friends quiz me every so often, I continued to met with my tutor and my professor after class, heck I even prayed the day of the exam that if it be God's will that he allow me to pass the final exam and pass the class.

The day of the final exam I woke up feeling great and feeling confident then ever that I was going to pass and move on to the final level of math classes College Math. I was one of the first person to show up to class and to get their exam, I took my time on each and every question not moving on until I was sure I had the right answer. I finished the exam and was one of the every last people to turn in their exam, Heck I'm pretty sure I was the last person to turn in their exam. The professor graded my exam and I sat down and waited. The professor called me up to her desk and gave me my graded final exam. I had failed the exam by just two percentage points.

I begged and I pleaded with the professor to please just give me those two percentage points so that I could pass. She looked me in my eyes and said, "If I give you a passing grade, You're just going to go onto College Math where you're going to struggle even more. And you only have one more semester left before you graduate so you'd only have one shot to get College Math right. You struggled to pass Basic Math, you struggled to pass this class. What kind of professor would I be if I let you go to the next level just to fail and watch all your friends graduate without you?" My heart became so heavy, I swear I thought it would drop down and come out my butt. I got on my bicycle and rode back to my condo ignoring everyone I saw that I knew on the way.

I got to my condo and I went inside, I went up to my room where Darrell was sitting on his side of the room and he asked me, "So did you pass?" I threw my books across my side of the room onto my bed and said, "Nope, That's it, I'm going home!" Tears filled my eyes and I threw myself on my bed and continued to cry. The school had soon sent me a letter that I was being academically dismissed from the school for "failure to met graduate requirements" and that I'd have to be out of my condo within the next month. Three months before I would have graduated and it was game over for me. I enjoyed spending the next moment I could with my friends and roommates saying my goodbyes before my mom would come pick me up and take me back to my childhood home where she still resided with John at the time.

I truly believe this was when my anxiety disorder truly surfaced as I became very depressed during this time. I truly believe I was a failure because I had failed at my dream of going to college for Graphic Design and getting my degree in Graphic Design. I labeled myself and honestly believed for the next two years that I was indeed a failure. Eventually after coming home from college I decided I would try to get my own Graphic Design small business off the ground. The first name I came up with was JM Design, I know how original right, use your first and last initial and add what your business is for and bam you got your business name. I'd eventually change it to something a little more original, ColorPool, Yes just like that capital C and capital P all one word.

I even changed my slogan from "Satisfaction Guaranteed" to "Turning Dreams Into Reality!" The idea for ColorPool actually came from an assignment in college where we had to come up with logo designs for a "fictitious company" and the best part was this was a class that was taught by the professor who I mentioned had said, "Idea's are like s fart, They come quick and some of the stink!" My logo for ColorPool was the design my professor had liked the most and had chosen for me to use in my final project which is to then create an identity for that "fictitious company." So ColorPool had gone from being an idea for fictitious company for a project in college to a actual real life company. I had business cards made and everything for ColorPool, I even had a cool banner made that I hung in my "office" at my house where I did business. Though most of my "clients" where of course family who supported me I did have a few "clients" who weren't family members.

Here's the thing though about doing business for friends and family. They say the are supportive of what your doing but then should you actually do any work for them, They expect a discount or for you to do it for free because your related or because your bro's or homies. Or they just "forget" to pay you or make some excuse why they can't pay you in the end and then you lose money. And when your business loses money, you lose money, and when you lose money, you got to dip into your own pockets to keep the ship a float. And doing that only works out until you eventually can't afford to do so anymore.

But that's not the only thing that killed ColorPool. What ultimately put the final nail in the coffin for ColorPool was the COVID-19 Pandemic. Having to shut down for the period when many business were required to close for hurt me badly. After business were able to resume business during the pandemic I was hurting for money when it came to my business finances and I wasn't getting any work and I had to dip into my business finances during the time business had to be closed so that I could make ends meet and survive the pandemic. Making the decision to close ColorPool was one of the hardest decision I ever had to make. It meant I personally had to make the decision to to admit I had failed to get ColorPool off the ground. It was the only dream I had left and like every other dream I had in life it shattered before my eyes!

ColorPool was my pride and joy, When I say I designed everything for it right down to the logo, I mean everything right down to the logo. I designed the logo, I came up with the slogan, I designed my business cards, I designed the banner I had, and all the marketing products I had like pens and t-shirts guess what, I designed those. Heck I even designed a website for ColorPool and I even managed said website. I created an email address and made my voicemail on my cellphone sound professional and include leaving messages for my business. I had really thought that I was going to make this small business work without having a Graphic Design degree. But when it was all said and done ColorPool claimed to do what I obviously couldn't, and that was to turn the idea of ColorPool into a reality.

Would I take going college back and spending those two years at college, No! I don't for a second regret my decision to go to college and chase my dream of a degree in Graphic Design because I'd be lying if I said I didn't learn anything from it, And I'd really be lying if I said I didn't benefit anything from it. I gained friendships and memories that will last a lifetime even if someone them are negative like drinking as much as I did an smoking as much as I did and worrying more about partying then I did studying and my education. Though I lost contact with Kelsi once I deleted my Facebook and Twitter accounts and after hearing Maggie graduated from the school and then not hearing from her after that, I still fallow David on Instagram and occasionally comment on his posts. Jonathan, Khiary, Darrell, Ashley and Josh I follow all them on Instagram and occasionally comment on their posts. They're all still making music Jonathan just released an album recently title Bean and it's really good.

Ashley has a brand he runs called Love More Bmore, you can find out more about that at www.lovemorebmore.com. Darrell, Khiary and Josh have just been kind of living life lately not much going on with them. I went to a Baltimore Ravens game back in October at M&T Bank Stadium in Baltimore as a birthday present and I wanted to meet up with all of them and spend some time catching up with them but didn't get to because I totally forgot to tell them I was going to be in Baltimore that day. So when I went back to Baltimore a couple months later I planned to meet up with them outside the stadium but things came up on their end and they were unable to meet up with me. So it's still on the bucket list to meet up with them and spend some time catching up with them. It'll happens someday and when it does it's going to be a great time with probably a lot of reminiscing about our days at The Art Institute of York – Pennsylvania.

<u>*Chapter 7*</u>

MENTAL HEALTH MATTERS

*"Peace is what I leave with you; it's my own peace
that I give to you. I do not give it as the world does.
Do not be worried and upset; do not be afraid."*
- John 14:27

Before we dive into this chapter I would just like to put a little trigger warning as this chapter I talk about my anxiety disorder and how I use to self harm. I also talk about suicide and suicidal tendencies. If you are triggered by talk of self harm or cutting specifically please skip past this chapter. I'd hate to find out that by you reading this portion of my book it caused you to relapse in your recovery or that it triggered you in any way shape or form. If you or anyone you know struggles with these things please seek help and know that there are people who love you and care about you as well as people who want to help you and guide you back to a healthier path for your life.

Ask I stated before my college roommates and I had a very good friendship among us. We would pick on each other all in the name of good fun and joke around all the time. But one time things went a little to far back in 2011, They guys kept trying locked me in my room and said they'd let me out if I said, "I love John." Yes, John my moms boyfriend at the time, the one I said I started off getting a long great with but then things went south between us. I felt in this moment like they were bullying me instead of innocently picking on me and became very upset. They eventually let me out of the room when they realize I was very upset.

I ran to the kitchen grabbed the sharpest knife we had and then went into the laundry closet and hid behind the washer and dryer toying with the idea of killing myself. I was crying and just looking at the knife trying to mustard up the confidence to end it all. They guys were looking for me and eventually checked the laundry closet and found me. They apologized to me and told me they didn't mean to upset me and asked me to come out of the laundry closet. I came out and they were shocked when they saw I had a knife with me and they again apologized for taking things to far in our fun and games of innocently joking around. They never took things that far again after that night and even made sure they never crossed that line with me again.

I feel like to a point I've always struggled with anxiety ever since I was young due to the fact I've always kind of feared the worst in things. Also I feel like being bullied as a kid didn't really help things either. But it wasn't until I was academically dismissed from college and labeled myself a failure before I'd be officially doctor diagnosed in 2013 with Generalized Anxiety Disorder, also know as G.A.D for short. My family doctor diagnosed me with it and placed me on medication for it. I knew a little bit about mental illnesses as when I was in high school I found out about the organization To Write Love On Her Arms, TWLOHA. Every year they did this thing where they'd encourage people to write the word LOVE on their arm and go about their day like that to spread awareness for suicide.

After being diagnosed with G.A.D I pretty much just went on living my life the best I could. One day I was on social media, I believe it was Facebook and I saw that the band Skillet had posted something about a Sick Of It Fan Photo Contest. The rules were simple, Take a photo of you holding a sign with something you are sick of and Submit that photo to be entered into the contest for a chance to be featured in Skillets fan lyric music video for their song Sick Of It. I had absolutely no expectation of even doing well in the contest but couldn't refuse the opportunity to enter as I was a big fan of Skillet and still am to this day. I submitted a photo of me holing a sign with the word FAILURE on it. This was me making it public that I truly and honestly believed that I was nothing more then a failure. I didn't even smile in the photo I took, not even a slight grin.

The contest began and the first round came and went and I received an email from the contest. The email was to congratulate me on making it through to the next round. As the rounds came and went I kept getting emails congratulating me on making it to the next round of the contest. After the round prior to the final round I received an email that congratulated me on making it to the final round of the contest and that if my photo was one of only

The photo I submitted into the Skillet Sick Of It Fan Lyric Music Video Contest.

ninety one photo's chosen in the final round I would have my photo be featured in the fan lyric music video for Skillets song Sick Of It. I couldn't believe it that I was only one round away from having my photo be featured in the music video. The final round ended and I received and email congratulating me once again, only this time it was to congratulate me on be one of the ninety one people selected worldwide to have their photo featured in the fan lyric music video for Skillets song Sick Of It.

The fan lyric music video came out and I watched it. I was smack dab in the exact middle of the music video. I couldn't believe it was real, But at the same time this gave me hope. This was what I needed to see that I wasn't a failure, Even though I failed college that doesn't make me a failure. Failing college didn't have to define who I am and feeling down on myself wasn't going to help anything either. This is the moment in time when I decided to go see my doctor regarding how I had been feeling and when he diagnosed me with Generalized Anxiety Disorder.

Eventually I would begin to have anxiety attacks at least once a week sometimes even multiple times a week. They got so bad that some days I'd have more then one a day. That is when things would get bad and boy did they get bad fast. My mental health go so bad during this time that I began to self harm. My method of choice when it came to self harming was carving, Carving is exactly like Cutting only instead of slicing yourself your cut words or symbols into yourself. Definitely wouldn't recommend doing this as it I never once felt good about the decision to do so after I did it.

When I would self harm I never cut myself really deep. I only ever cut myself to the point that I would start to bleed, So because of that I don't even have any scares from my time of cutting. I use to cut the back of my arm, Not my forearm like where your palm is then your wrist and that part of your hand but the back of your hand where most of the hair grows on your arm. The skin there is tougher so it was easier not to cut to far because their isn't any veins that run through that part of your arm. I carved words like Pain, Broken, Weak, etc into my arm just deep enough that blood would begin to seep out and then I'd wrap it up with a gauze pad or something. If anyone asked me what happened I would tell them, "Oh that, My cat scratched me." Everyone knew I had a cat and everyone knew I loved my cat and would always play around with my cat and torment him in good fun so it was a lie that was believable.

Xeno (cat) and I

When I would self harm most of the time it would happen after I had a few beers or alcoholic drinks as that would keep me from thinking clearly and talking myself out of doing it. I would usually play a song like Monsters by Shinedown or the cover of Zombies that Bad Wolves did back in 2018, but most of the time I would self harm listening to the song Ghost by Bad Flower. I chose that song most of the time because the lyrics matched how I felt in those moments. In the song it starts out, "I tried it once before but I didn't get to far, I felt a lot of pain but it didn't stop my heart, And all I really wanted was someone to give a little f**k, But I waited there forever and nobody even looked up." Then next part says, "I tried it once before and I think I mighta messed up, I struggled with the veins and I guess I didn't bleed enough, But maybe I'm alive cause I really didn't wanna die, But nothing very special ever happens in my life." That's exactly how I felt every time I would self harm, I did it because I just wanted people to see how I felt inside but I never had the intent to end my life when self harming.

At this time in my life I worked in a nursing home and rehabilitation center as a dietary cook. Also at this time the they began to hire teenagers like fifteen or sixteen your old's as dietary aids. One day one of the girls who was a dietary aid had asked me what happened to my arm? I told her, "Oh, My cat scratched me" She called my bluff and started telling me that I was a psychopath and threatening to have me admitted to a mental hospital. This didn't help my mental health any as it only made things worse because I already felt bad about cutting myself as I promised myself all my life that no matter what I'd never do something like that. Her friend who also worked there would even make fun of me telling me the same stuff and that I was weird.

Self Harming honestly made me feel so bad about myself because like I said I promised my self no matter how bad things got I'd never harm myself or try to kill myself. So one day after having two anxiety attacks and carving the word weak into my arm I called my mom crying. I told her about how I had two anxiety attacks and self harmed myself and that I wanted to go to the hospital. She asked me, "Do you want to go to the urgent care or the emergency room?" I told her I wanted to go to the emergency room. We got to the emergency room and I checked in and told them I was there for anxiety, The lady looked at my arm and asked if I had self harmed and I told her yes.

This was probably the shortest wait I've ever had in the emergency room as they brought me back to a room fairly quick. They had removed literally EVERYTHING that wasn't bolted down or part of the room from the room and made me remove my clothing and change into a disposable pair of pants and shirt that were about three or four sizes to big for me. I literally had to hold the pants up as the little sorry excuse of a draw string wouldn't even go tight enough to keep the pants up on me. They gave my mom and I folding chairs to sit on and a nurse had stationed herself outside of my room. I swear I'm not being over dramatic when I say every time I so much as coughed the slightest cough this lady would look up into the room and say, "Everything okay in there?" She was so on guard that it literally made me wish I was dead.

A doctor came in to take a look at my arm and he said, "Wow, I've never seen anyone cut themselves so strategically and well thought out before." I was like, "Who the heck says that to someone!" He cleaned up my arm and wrapped it up again and then told me the psychiatrist would be in soon to see me. The psychiatrist came in a began a psychic evaluation on me. Part way through the evaluation was the end of her shift so she pasted my evaluation on to a next psychiatrist who was coming on duty to re-leave her. He came in and claimed the previous psychiatrist didn't give him any notes so we had to start the evaluation all over again.

I told him the same thing I told the previous psychiatrist, I did harm myself, I didn't want to harm anyone else and I didn't want to kill myself or anyone else. He left the room and then after some time came back and told me that he didn't feel I needed to be admitted to the hospital as an inpatient but only felt comfortable discharging me from the emergency room on the understanding that I was to complete an Intensive Outpatient Program where at the very least I'd be required to meet with and talk to a Behavior Health Councilor aka a Psychologist. He also told me that I was to follow up with my family doctor in the next two to three days. I followed up with my family doctor and told him how I was recently in the emergency room for my anxiety and self harming and he told me, "I don't like to increase medications or change medications if I absolutely don't have to." I was thinking to myself, "Dude, I was literally just in the hospital for carving words into my arm, What do I got to do hang myself from the ceiling fan in your office and let you watch as I spin around and around?" If being at the hospital for my anxiety wasn't reason to alter my medication in someway I didn't know what was.

He never did do anything so I stopped seeing him altogether. Then I began to meet with a Psychologist, She was alright, Kind of annoying though because everything I said she had some way to relate to it with a story from her life that I genuinely didn't care about. She in formed me that while I was in the Intensive Outpatient Program that I was unable to do any drugs or alcohol or that'd be a violation of the programs policies and she'd be required to report any and all violations to the hospital beings they were the ones who where requiring me to take part in the program. I spent the next five months meeting with and talking with the Psychologist. She at one point asked me about doing group therapy and I told her that I really didn't want to do group therapy so she didn't make me do it. Five months later after reducing our visits from twice a week to once a week and then once a week going well she had informed me that she felt I made a lot of progress and that there was nothing she could do for me further.

She requested for the hospital to allow me to be released from the program and they accepted her request so she discharged me from the program and wished me well. I was never so glad to be discharged in my life as I HATE talking about my feelings, especially to a stranger who makes a living off listening to me complain about my feelings. But I'd be lying if I said I didn't learn valuable information to help me cope and manage my anxiety. I even learned that I not only have Generalized Anxiety Disorder but my Generalized Anxiety Disorder comes with traits of Depression so that is why at times I have signs of Depression even though I was never diagnosed with a Depression Disorder of any kind. So in a way the Intensive Outpatient Program wasn't all bad and did pay off in the end. But I had no desire to ever have to go back to that place again.

Shortly after being released from the Intensive Outpatient Program I had left the church I had attended since I was 3 years old, Grace Fellowship Church of Ephrata, I had attended for a total of 25 years up to that point. I left because I just felt like I wasn't growing spiritually there anymore and that if had nothing left to offer me. So I started attending the church my mom left the church we attended since I was 3 years old for, Reamstown Church Of God. I played Softball for Grace Fellowship from 2013 to 2017, 2017 was the last year the church had a team as after that year for some reason everyone or most of the people on that team at the time started attending other churches. So in 2019 after not having a Softball team to play of at church for the past two years I started attending Reamstown Church Of God right after their Softball season that year had ended and they won the league Championship. I remember the Sunday they all got on stage and announced they had won the Championship, They just looked like a Championship team

Me batting for Reamstown Church Of God in my first season in 2020.

standing there proud of each other with a sense of accomplishment on their faces.

It was at that moment I knew I wanted to be a part of that team as well. So the next season I signed up to join the team after two years of not playing at all. I remember the first Sunday service I went to after deciding to relocate to Reamstown Church Of God as my choice place of worship I was so moved and over come by the whole spirit during the praise and worship time that I began to get emotional, I said down and buried my head in my lap and began to cry. My mom asked me what was wrong handing me a tissue, I said, "It's my freaking anxiety!" I had never cried in church before. It happened a few times after that but I eventually learned that it's okay to let your emotions flow in church, There's absolutely nothing wrong with it.

I've been attending Reamstown Church Of God for a couple of years now and have absolutely no intentions of leaving the church any time soon. I just finished my third softball season with Reamstown Church Of God though I was out for the season after our second game of the season after breaking 2.5 milometers of the back of my 5th metatarsal aka little toe. I landing wrong doing a board slide down a hand railing at the skate park on my skateboard in the time between our second and third game of the 2023 season. Before that I hadn't been out for the season since 2016 when I played for Grace Fellowship Church of Ephrata which I'll talk about more in depth in the next chapter. I still am growing spiritually through attending Reamstown Church Of God and have even started attending the men's group, Forge, every Sunday evening as well as attending the Encounter Service the first Sunday evening of every month.

I started training to be a referee in professional wrestling on the independent circuit in November of 2018 and in March 2019 I began working shows as ringside security and then in August of 2019 refereed my first match on my first show. Before every show I always had the absolute worst anxiety ever. About a year before I started training to be a referee with Atomic Championship Wrestling in at that time Stevens, Pennsylvania I attended a show as a fan. The featured Superstar at that show was none other then the "Scream Queen" Daffney. I was so excited as Daffney is one of my all time favorite female wrestlers, Her time teaming with MsChief as the Scream Queens and her time managing the team of David Flair and Crowbar are my favorite memories of her in ring career. So when she came to ACW I knew I had to meet her and I had to get a picture with her as well as her autograph.

I met her and got my picture with her as well as an autograph, She was so cool and a truly genuine down to earth person. On September 1st, 2021 Daffney went live on Instagram and I decided to watch. She was talking about how she was struggling mentally and just couldn't continue anymore and how she has this brain condition you get from multiple concussions and how doctors don't know much about this condition because they haven't had the opportunity to really research it so she wanted to donate her brain to science. She then showed a gun on her live and the cut the live off. I knew exactly what she was about to do but I didn't know her personally so I couldn't reach out to her. I do know some people who did and received no answer from Daffney.

The next day it was confirmed that Shannon Spruill aka Daffney has taken her own life. I immediately broke down upon hearing the news as I knew from watching her live that she was going to take her life as she even read a suicide note on the live. I reached out to a few of the people I know who were close to her and offered my condolences to them. I took her autograph and I put it in a frame and I have her autograph displayed in my home to pay my respects to a women who inspired me to get into the industry and who provided me with many great memories of her doing what she loved in the ring.

R.I.P Daffney Unger
09/01/2021

Every year since I think about what life would be like if Daffney was still here on this earth and often wonder what it would have been like to referee one of her match. I never thought the death of a professional wrestler would impact me so much but it honestly makes me sad every time I look at her autographed picture I have of her and I think, "If only I could have been able to help in someway."

Before that though in June of 2018 one of the superstars who worked for Atomic Championship Wrestling Rockin' Rebel took his own life after a dispute with his wife that ended with him taking the life of his wife. Like I said previously I began working ACW shows as in ring security in March 2018 so I worked the March, April and May show that year with Rockin' Rebel. I had also been attending ACW shows since the summer of 2015 and became a fan of Rockin' Rebel and had a few conversations with him during intermission. He was also a genuine stand up guy who would give you the best advice as far as in ring stuff was concerned. When I heard he had taken his wife's life and then taken his own life thereafter I couldn't believe it, I remember that show ACW held in June 2018 them calling everyone out from the back to surround the ring for a ten bell salute, This would be my first ten bell salute as a worker of the professional wrestling industry. Rockin' Rebel is another reason I decided to get involved in the professional wrestling industry.

I bring up the deaths of Rockin' Rebel and Daffney not to throw shade of what they did or open sealed wounds of the people who loved them dearest. I bring their deaths up because I would have never been able to tell you that outside the venue that Rockin' Rebel was having issues at home and that Daffney was hurting on the inside to the point she would take her own life. Mental Illness isn't always visible or obvious. Be kind to everyone because you don't know when will be the last time that you see them and remember your life matters and there is people who care and love you. Also check on your loved ones and the people you cherish and let them know it's okay to not be okay, but it's important to talk about how your feeling.

Before I end this chapter I would just like to say that as I said in the beginning of this chapter, If you or a loved one are struggling with your mental health please seek help. Please also remember that you matter to someone in someway, There are people who love you and would absolutely be torn to pieces if you weren't here or something happened to you. I referenced that song Ghost by Bad Flower and how I related to it in my times of self harming and now I'd like to reference the chorus of that song, it says, "Take the blade away from me, I'm a freak, I am afraid that, All the blood escaping me won't end the pain, And I'll be haunting all the lives that cared for me, I died to be the white ghost, Of the man that I was meant to be." The term, White Ghost, comes derives from Hungarian Mythology and is referred to as "the ghost of usually a girl or young woman that died violently; usually from suicide, murder, or imprisonment." Also in the beginning of the music video for Ghost by Bad Flower is a quote by an Unknown person that states, "Suicide doesn't end the chances of life getting worse. It eliminates the possibility of it ever getting better."

My struggles with my mental health even encouraged me to become trained to be a Mental Health Peer and later a Mental Health Mentor through iPrevail Health. I went to iPrevail Health's website seeking help for my mental health as a way to help manage my mental health after being released from the Intensive Outpatient Program. I learned about Cognitive Behavioral Therapy which I learned a little about in the Intensive Outpatient Program as well so I kind of already knew what I was learning. I completed what iPrevail calls the User Program and was able to then take part in the Peer Coaching Program where I was able to learn how to talk with other users on the website and how to help them through talking with them and learning about the resources that iPrevail offers to it's users. After completing the Peer Program I was able to move on to the Mentor Program where I learned how to better assist the people I would talk to and how to be a mentor to them. This meant that they could request to speak to me specifically instead of to the first person available.

I received no monetary compensation for this. They closest thing to being paid for this that I received was that if I talked with a certain number of people per month the monthly subscription fee for me to subscribe to iPrevail's services on the website would be waved. I also received reward points for completing sections of the program I was in and for the hours and sessions I spent talking with users as a mentor that I could later redeem for Amazon gift cards. Honestly though just the satisfaction of knowing I helped someone feel better about themselves or their lives was compensation enough in my mind. I have a passion for helping others and I always have to the point that sometimes I forget to help myself or put myself on a the back burner just to help someone else.

If you or someone you know is in crisis contact the Suicide Prevention Lifeline at 1-800-273-TALK (8255), or dial 911 in the case of an emergency!

Chapter 8

"*DON'T LET ME DIE!*"

*"Do not be discouraged, for the Lord
your God will be with you wherever you go."
- Joshua 1:9*

My friend Chandler was selling his 1999 Oldsmobile Intrigue, I needed a car as I had wrecked the Subaru Legacy I had so I no longer had a car. Chandler made me a deal to buy his car and I was so happy. It was a forest green color and didn't look bad for being like 17 years old, It had no radio though so I had to buy a radio for it. I remember the first thing I did with that car was of course gave it the zero to sixty test and it did it in a respectable four or five seconds. I had to take it to get inspected though as the inspection was out of date. It passed inspection but the emissions didn't pass so the garage refused to put a new inspection sticker on it.

I had planned to do the work needed to have it pass but I continued to drive it even though the inspection remained out of date. Chandler was a professional wrestler on the independent circuit under the name "The Caribbean Superstar" CJ Cruz. I started going to independent professional wrestling shows about almost a year prior to this time when Chandler had asked me if I could drive him to a show he had with Regional Championship Wrestling in Reading, Pennsylvania. I agreed and I was excited to show him the new radio I put in the car I bought from him, It wasn't anything special it was a black radio with blue trim a Pioneer radio I got from Walmart for like twenty bucks and didn't even have it screwed in place yet just had it plugged up and sitting in the radio slot of the center dash consul of the car. I picked up Chandler and his friend BJ and I believe if memory serves me correctly our friend Brian also was booked for the same show so I picked him up as well. His gimmick was pretty cool, His name was Scarecrow, He had this mask made out of a burlap sack and he would laugh like the Joker from Batman.

We got into Reading a little early so we grabbed a bit to eat at a WAWA gas station near the venue. We sat in the car eating our food and laughing and having a good time. Brian was doing his family guy impersonations of Stewie and Brian the dog which were always hilarious. After we were done eating we headed to the venue. I was excited for the show because the featured superstar to appear was none other then J.J Dillon the manager of the infamous professional wrestling stable back in the 80's and 90's the Four Horsemen compiled of Ric Flair, Arn Arnderson, Ole Anderson and Tully Blanchard. Chandler and Brain went backstage and BJ and I found our seat in the front row as I always bought VIP tickets when I went to an independent professional wrestling show because they were usually only twenty or twenty five dollars sometimes cheaper depending on the promotion and location of the show.

When I saw JJ Dillon at his table in the merchandise area of the venue I went over to meet him. I bought a photo oh him and the Four Horsemen from a photo shoot they had back in the day and asked JJ if he could autograph it for me. He autographed the photo where he was standing in the photo and even put it in a protective sleeve along with a business card and a certificate of authenticity. I took my autograph and went back to my seat and waited for the show to start. The show was great as they usually are. And afterwards we got back into my car and headed for home.

It was almost midnight by the time I had gotten everyone home, I dropped Brian off first and then BJ and finally Chandler. Then I began to head home towards my house, I was feeling good, I had the windows rolled down and the music up full blast. Then about three miles from home it hit me like a truck, I got tired out of absolutely nowhere. I started dozing off behind the wheel and when I caught myself and opened my eyes my car was heading towards the drainage ditch on the side of the road. I tried to pull out of it and back onto the road but it was to late. I had hit the concrete casing of where the drainage pipe was head on with my car doing sixty miles per hour.

This is where my car hit, flipped and rolled.

My car went head over heals over the drainage pipe and landed on it's roof and then rolled over on it's size. The air bags deployed and everything inside my car, I knew it was bad as the dashboard had crunched down onto my lap and I couldn't get out of the car. I felt around what I thought was the floor of the car for my cellphone to call for help not realize the car was upside down and what I thought was the floor was actually the roof of the car. After a while of no luck I had given up and decided to just lay there as I was beginning to go into shock from my injuries. Eventually a passer by had seen my car on the side of the road on his side and realize that wasn't normal and decide to investigate to see if anyone was inside. When they realized I was in the car they called for help.

The next thing I know I heard the voice of a woman asking if I could hear her, I replied, "I don't want to die, Please don't let me die!" She said, "I'm not going to let you die, I'm a police officer, I need to know are you okay?" I relied again, I'd don't want to die, Please don't let me die!" She then again reassured me that she wasn't going to let me die and then asked if I had been drinking anything. And once again all I could say was, "I don't want to die, Please don't let me die!" By that time the local fire department had arrived and I heard a mans voice said, "I need you to cover your entire face with both your hands, We are going to break the glass to get you out of the car."

I did as I was instructed and then felt the glass shatter. When they realized I was trapped in the car by how the car crunched on impact they had called for the rescue squad to help get me out. Once I was out of the car they immediately put me onto a stretcher and cut my clothing off and loaded me into a nearby ambulance. I don't remember anything after that until I woke up staring at a ceiling that looked an awful lot like that of the hospital. A women had looked over me and said, "You were involved in a car wreck, Who can we call?" I asked what time it was and the lady said, "It's one in the morning."

I said to her, "Well you and I are the only ones dumb enough to be awake at this time of night and clearly I'm no good at it so who do you call." She said, "There has to be someone we can call to let them know you are here." I told her she could call my mom and my sister who both worked second shift, So they were sleeping at the time. I don't remember anything after that until I woke up in a hospital room and had to pee really badly. I called for the nurse and she came in and asked what I needed. I told her I have to pee really badly and she informed that I have a catheter in and that I could just go.

A doctor had come in some time later and told me

that my injuries included a bruised heart, bruised lungs, fluid in my lungs, four broken ribs, internal bleeding, and that I lost a total of two liters of blood in the car crash and required four blood transfusions upon my arrival to the hospital in order to save my life. He also informed me that the tube I had sticking out of my side was a chest tube and that it was to drain the fluid from my lungs and the blood from my insides. After the doctor left a few hours later the hospital had notified me that my sister had received the message they left on her voicemail and that she had called my moms and that my mom was on her way into the hospital. My mom arrived at the hospital and when she saw me laying in the hospital bed she broke down in tears as any mother would upon seeing her child laying helpless in a hospital bed. The next morning I was flooded with visitors including Chandler who was taking the news about my car crash hard. He was blaming himself saying he should have never sold me that car.

I assured him it wasn't his fault unless he rigged the car with sleeping gas or something like that that would have caused me to fall asleep and crash. Also my neighbor Doug who had asked me the day of my car crash to take him to the casino but I told him I couldn't cause of having to take Chandler to his show had visited as well and kept saying how if I had just taken him to the casino that night this never would have happened because he wouldn't have let me fall asleep behind the wheel.

A couple days later my dad came to visit and had brought me my mail. Included in my mail was a letter from the police, It was a fine for Reckless Driving and I had ten days to send in my plea of guilty or not guilty. I began to cry and my dad asked what was wrong so I showed him the letter. He told me, "Don't worry about it, I'll deal with it!" I plead guilty and gave the letter to my dad, The next day he came in and told me everything was taken care of. He had paid the fine and told the police exactly what he thought of them giving me a fine as I lay in the hospital fighting for my life.

While I was in the hospital there were these two girls around my age who I noticed had stopped in front of my room and were looking in my room. These two girls then sneaked into my room and told me that I didn't know them but they saw that I was about their age and they wanted to pray for me. I accepted their offer for pray and they prayed over me. They then informed me that they were there to visit their grandpa who was in the room next to mine and that he had fallen down the stairs. I thanked them for their prayers and wished their grandpa well in his recovery and they left before anyone realized they were in my room. This was how I knew that God had been with me during my car crash because everyone from the police to the firefighters to the EMT's, the doctors at the hospital, heck even myself couldn't believe nor could they understand how I managed to be alive.

I spent a week in the Intensive Care Unit healing from my injuries. They were going to let me leave after six days but I had to stay an extra twenty four hours for observation due to the fact that when they removed the chest tube that I had my lungs began to collapse. Finally when I was able to go home I had called my sister to bring me home, My sister arrived and as I walked out with my sister the doctors and nurses began to congratulate me and say how thankful they were that I pulled through. This confused me so I began to ask why they were congratulating me, they said, "You're going to be a father!" My sister was about eight months pregnant at this time so it was pretty obvious. I said, "This is my sister" and they were all like, "Well still you're going to be an uncle!"

My sister brought me home and I couldn't even go up to my bed room as it was on the third floor and the doctor at the hospital wasn't even keen on me having to go up steps to get into my house on the second floor but discharged me with the understanding that once I got into my apartment I was to stay there and to stay on the second floor. I was to have a friend or family member bring cloths and whatever else I needed down to the second floor for me. So I spent my time recovering on the couch in my living room and Jared and Paul had helped me as far as getting cloths from my bedroom and down to the second floor so I could change every day into fresh cloths. My sister came over everyday to help me care for the wound from where I had my chest tube. My family did a great job at providing meals for me to eat and making sure I had everything I needed to recover comfortably. My landlord even told me not to worry about my portion of the rent and to focus on recovering and getting myself healthy again.

After I recovered I went back to living my life as normal until about six months later when I would start having breathing complications. I went to my family doctor and he said to me, "I hope you didn't drive here?" I said, "No, why?" He told me that he was calling me an ambulance and that I was going to the hospital because I had fluid surrounding my heart. So the ambulance came and took me to the hospital where upon arrival I had a chest catheter inserted into my chest to drain the fluid out of my heart. All I could do was lay there and let the fluid drain out of my heart.

At one point the fluid stopped draining from my heart but there was still fluid around my heart that needed to be drained out so the doctor who was on third shift said to me, "I'm going to do something that is very illegal and could result in me losing both my job and my doctors license, So I need you to promise me you won't try to get out of bed on your own or roll out of bed." I promised him and he began to raise my hospital bed as high as it went, I swear that thing was a good six to eight feet off the ground at least. He told me he was going to let me like that all night and that he'd be back in before the first shift arrived to lower my bed so no one would know. About five in the morning he came back in a lowered my bed, He looked a the bag where the fluid drained to and he said, "WOW, That worked better then I thought it would, We might do that again tonight!" And that's exactly what he did the next night. After spending another week in the hospital I was discharged from the hospital the day before Thanksgiving.

This breathing thing was used to help strengthen my lungs again.

Ever since my car wreck I haven't been able to drive a car by myself without having an anxiety attack. Ever since that day every time I get behind the wheel of a car without anyone else being in the car I get so anxious I begin shaking. Jared and I were out one time after my car wreck riding motorcycles, Jared was on his Kawasaki Ninja and I was on my Vento Zip 50cc motor scooter. His motorcycle had broke down so he gave me his keys and told to go back to the house and gets his pickup truck and drive it to where he was broken down at. So that's what I did but when I got home and got behind the wheel of his pick up truck that was two years after my car wreck and the first thought that went through my head was, "Wow, The last time I drove a can with four wheels I nearly died." I had to take about five minutes to collect myself before I was able to fire up his pick up truck and be on my way.

Another time Jared had bought a new motorcycle and needed someone to drive his car back as he drove his new motorcycle home. He asked me if I would do it and I agreed knowing driving a car made me uncomfortable and still at the time trigger my anxiety. We went to leave the lot of the place Jared bought his new motorcycle from and I had to spend about five minutes to collect myself and settle down as I was shaking from my anxiety being so high. Jared had already pulled out of the lot and eventually came back and said, "Dude, What are you doing?" I told him I just had to get my anxiety in check and that I'd be good. After a while we were able to leave the lot and start our journey home.

Once we hit the highway Jared began to punch it full throttle down the highway on his new motorcycle and as he pulled further and further from me I toyed with the thought of putting the peddle to the metal in his car and I did a little bit but quickly became very uncomfortable and over come with anxiety. I remember we stopped at a gas station on the way home and I told Jared about how I wasn't really comfortable going as fast as we were and he told me, "You're doing fine, Just don't crash." I know he was just trying to be encouraging but it's easy to say "Just don't crash" it's another thing to not crash. We eventually got home no problem and I said to myself, "Good now hopefully I don't have to do this again for a while." Even to this day as I'm writing this book the thought of even driving a car or a truck makes me highlight uncomfortable and when I tell people hoe driving makes me uncomfortable nobody can seem to understand why.

When something almost takes your life especially when it very well should have taken your life, That creates a fear in the person that event effected. I creates a trigger that causes that person to relive the feelings and the memories of the event that is link to their fear and it causes that person to become uncomfortable or anxious, etc. I can drive a motor scooter, heck I can even drive a motorcycle to this day but ask me to drive a car or a truck and you can forget about it. I tell people the first car accident I had was like the one I mentioned in this chapter, only that one my car slide off the road as I was going around a turn at a normal speed. I didn't flip over the concrete barrier though as I wasn't speeding, I walked away from that crash perfectly fine. But this last car accident damn near killed me and it very well should have so why would I drive a car again only to have the same thing happen a third time.

I guarantee you I almost died last time, the third time will be the time that I do end up dead. When I think back to how the only thing I could say in that moment as I laid in my car helpless was, "I don't want to die, Please don't let me die" and how it baffled literally everyone involved how I survived that crash that's what scares the absolute crap out of me, even to this day. I'd rather walk ten thousand miles to get to where I need to be before ever getting behind the wheel of a car or truck again. I don't know if this fear will last forever, Or if it'll be one that I can eventually find victory over but all I know is people don't seem to understand how this even has played a massive part on my life and they are very ignorant towards me regarding it. Most people tell me, "Why don't you just get a car" or "I don't see why you can't just get a car" or some ignorant statement like that that discredits and invalidates all the feelings I have stemming from my near fatal car wreck. But I promise you this, Little do they know none of those statements are going to help me feel any better about the thought of driving a car again, nor will they get me to drive a car again. If anything Jared's

Damage from my first car wreck where I just slide off the road.

little hey I bought a new motorcycle can you drive my car home for me stints will help me over come my fear more then anything as it allows me to see I am capable of driving a car without wrecking it and that things can be fine and go alright when I'm behind the wheel of a car.

One wish I do have from my car wreck is that I wish I could get a hold of the person who realized when seeing my car on the side of the road and came to see if anyone was inside, I genuinely wish and hope that person is blessed beyond belief even up to this day and for the rest of their life. I also wish I would be able to get a hold of the police officer who arrived on the scene and kept talking to me to keep me awake and alert so that I wouldn't die. All I know is from the name on the ticket I got was that her name was Officer Fox. I did find out that in 2021 Officer Fox had retired from the police force so obviously she is happy with how her career as a police officer turned out. I truly hope that she to is blessed beyond belief and that she is enjoying her life as she is now retired and can spend her time with family and friends and loved ones. I really wish thought that I could tell her just how much she means to me and my life and how grateful I am for her service, especially on the night I wrecked my car as if it wasn't for her I might just have died in that car wreck.

I also am thankful and grateful for the nurses and the doctors at the hospital working the Intensive Care Unit that night. Without them I never would have survived my injuries. This night honestly gave me a whole new respect for healthcare professionals. I remember the one night they had Lemon Butter Cod for dinner and the nurse brought me my tray. I ate everything on my tray per usual except for the Lemon Butter Cod. The nurse had asked me if I was feeling alright and why I didn't eat my fish, I told her because it looks like a used dish sponge, and she offered to get me a sandwich in place of it.

I also am thankful for those two girls who sneaked into my room to talk with me and to pray over me. I truly believe they were angels sent by God as a sign to show me that he was with me through the entire thing and that he wasn't going to leave me or forsake me at any point along the way. Those girls really impacted me to continue to fight the good fight to recover from my injuries. I genuine hope they're grandpa recovered and that they are doing well in life where ever they may be and that they to are blessed beyond belief. It's amazing how a simple thing like two people you don't even know taking the time to do something as simple as pray for you, a stranger, could impact your life so greatly.

Another thing that impacted my life from that day on and even changed my life eventually was the pastor of Reamstown Church Of God, The pastor came to visit me in the hospital even though at the time I didn't attend the church, I was still attending Grace Fellowship at that time. This was a huge reason why when I decided to relocate churches why I decided to attend Reamstown Church Of God. It would have been so easy for him to say, "Sure this guys mom attends my church, but he does not so therefore I'm not going to waste my time visiting him." I don't even think I've ever told him to this day that because of him visiting me in the hospital and praying over me that was a factor that played into me eventually attending the church that he was the pastor of. It really is little things like that, that can impact you more then you even realize. So as you can see thankfulness and gratefulness are two things that I learned from this experience. Thought this experience was one I'd rather never experience again, If I could go back and avoid it ever happening I think I'd honestly have to pass over the opportunity to do so.

Chapter 9

JESUS IS MY SAVIOR, NOT MY RELIGION

"For God so loved the world that he gave
his only son, that whoever believes in him
should not parish but have everlasting life."
- John 3:16

I just want to take a moment, Well a chapter to take the focus off of myself and focus on the person who I truly do owe my life to. To the person who without them I'd most likely be one of two places right now other then writing this book and that being either in jail or in a grave six feet under ground somewhere. I want to talk about Christ for a moment. Christ has been a vital part of my life as I'm sure you can tell from everything you've read up to this point. From a young age I was taught the importance and the benefits of a healthy relationship with Christ. There's a saying that goes, "Jesus Is My Savior, Not My Religion."

If you live your life viewing Jesus as your religion you're not going to find you have a healthy relationship with Christ. Jesus wants to have a full blown relationship with you. He knows how many hairs are on your head and he knows every moment of your life even before it happens. He knows where you'll be five years from now and he even knows weather or not you'll eventually give your life to him. He knows every thought you have, He see's every tear you cry and he see's every time you fall. Jesus wants to be a major part of your life but he's not going to force you to make him a major part of your life or a part of your life at all.

God sent his son Jesus as a baby to this earth to live a human life. Jesus know his assignment even before he got to this earth. He know he would walk the earth preaching the gospel of the Lord God his father in Heaven only to be beaten and nailed to a cross at the age of thirty three. Now if you tell me, "Hey go do this, Oh and by the way it's going to lead to you dying in one of the most humiliating ways known to man." I'm going to tell you, "You can go eat a bag of rocks!" But Jesus didn't argue or try to dispute his assignment, He went willingly.

Jesus chose not to align himself with the most popular of people either. His disciples where mostly Fishermen or Tax Collectors. I've gone fishing, Never in a boat like the disciples probably did but I find fishing to be absolutely boring. Who spends their day sitting in or by a body of water with a pole and some string trying to catch one of the most brain dead animals on this planet. And then there's the Tax Collectors, I'll look you straight in your eyes and tell you to your face that you're a bold faced liar if you try and tell me you enjoy filing your taxes year after year after year. Jared's mom files taxes for a living and I just think to myself, "Why would anyone choose to file taxes for a living?

But again these are the people Jesus chose to be his disciples and to follow him. So this is proof that Christ uses even the most hated people in the world to carry out his work through. Nobody is off limits when it comes to Christ using someone for a certain purpose or for Christ to get something done. Jesus was challenged his entire life when it came to his work here on earth. People refused to believe he was the son of God and that he could preform miracles. When he did perform miracles he was viewed as some kind of wizard or sorcerer.

If I was Jesus I would have packed my bags and said, "Father, I'm done with this crap, I want to come home right now, I hate it here!" But he didn't give up ever, He continue to carry out the mission of his work healing the sick and saving the lives of those who gave him the time to hear his message and devoted their lives to him through hearing his message. Eventually when it came time for him to fulfill the final mission he had as a human being on this earth he did so without hesitation. For his "crime" of, Claiming To Be The Messiah, he was given the sentence of Crucifixion. Now crucifixion was in those times reserved for the most serious of crimes. Crucifixion was meant to be a way to humiliate a criminal for their crimes. And somehow by Jesus saying that he was The Messiah, The King Of The Jews, that was enough to label him one of the worst criminals in history at that time deeming it suitable for him to be crucified.

Now the other thing you must realize about crucifixion back in that time was that it wasn't a private affair, They didn't take you to a room or a secret yard to crucify you, No it was a public event like a concert or a parade in today's times. People came from all over to witness a good crucifixion back then. Jesus was tied up and beaten with a whip, It's believed he was whipped a total of thirty nine times because forty was the magic number used to kill a man and they didn't want to kill Jesus yet. They even cut his hair and tore his robe mocking him as they did so, Heck they even spit on him. They then placed a "crown" of thorns on his head and pushed it down until the thorns had pierced his head causing blood to drip down, He was then given the cross, the same cross he would be crucified on. He was then paraded through the streets, Publicly shamed and spit on even more along the way.

Some of his disciples were were even in attendance at one point Simon of Cyrene had to help Jesus as Jesus began struggling to carry the cross any further. Once they got to the sight where crucifixions took place they nailed Jesus to the cross and rose it up until it dropped into place in the ground. Jesus cross was in the middle of two others who where already crucified, Both men on either side of Jesus were thieves sentenced to crucifixion as well for their crimes. The thief on the right hand side of Jesus had asked Jesus at one point to remember him when Jesus went to Heaven. And Jesus did remember him as that thief entered into the Kingdom of Heaven after he had died. The thief on the left of Jesus he had joined the crowd and the soldiers in mocking Jesus on the cross so for that reason he did not enter into the Kingdom of Heaven after he had died.

Jesus even said as the soldiers nailed him to the cross, "Forgive them father for they know not what they do!" Jesus final words on the cross would be, "It is finished." After he had died he was taken off the cross and his body given a proper burial by being placed into a tomb. This was not common after crucifixion but was done for Jesus in respect for Jewish Law by Joseph of Arimathea. Three days after Jesus body had been place into the tomb, Mary Magdalene had come to his tomb to find the stone blocking the opening had been rolled away and the tomb had been empty. Mary then ran to tell Peter and John that Jesus tomb was empty and they ran to the tomb to see for themselves.

Christ appeared to Mary and later to the disciples to show them that he had risen from the dead like he previously told them he would. He eventually would ascend to Heaven to live there along with the Lord God, his Father. Now Christ didn't do all this because he wanted to know what it'd be like to be a human man or because he thought it'd be a cool idea. Christ endured all this because due to Adam and Eve disobeying God in the beginning of the world, Sin had entered the word as a result of that. Jesus would bare the sins of the world on his back during his crucifixion thus the reason the cross symbolizes our sins being forgiven. The moment Jesus died upon the cross all the sins of the world past, present and future sin would be forgiven and the opportunity to have eternal life through Christ and have a permanent place with him in Heaven upon our death would arise. That is why Jesus endured all that he endured while subjecting himself to a life of a mortal man on this earth. And that is why when I was 18 years old one night when I was at Crossfire, I had decided to rededicate my life to Christ again after previously doing so at age 15.

No matter what you do, Once you ask Christ into your heart there is no going back, There is not undoing it or any way you can lose Christ being in your life. I'll guide you through how to ask Christ into your heart and into your life later in the book so that after reading this book you to can have a permanent place in Heaven. In Heaven there will be no pain, no sorrow, no guilt or shame. Only positive vibes in Heaven. But now I'd like to talk about the opposite option of giving your life to Christ and having a place in Heaven. The opposite option is a life cast away from Christ into the fiery pits of Hell where it's pain and torture all day every day with no chance of things getting better.

Some people believe that Hell isn't real, That there is no such thing as Hell. I can tell you it's a very real place and you don't want to end up there, And I'm about to tell you just how I know it's a real place. One night in 2018 I journeyed through Hell, Now I know what you're thinking, "How have you been to Hell if one you're a Christian and two you're not dead?" I don't know if it was part of a nightmare or an out of body experience or what, All I know is when I woke up I was terrified and sweating bullets. I was in Hell and I knew it was hell because it was extremely hot, there was fire everywhere, and where there wasn't fire it looked like the inside of a cave. It was dark and I was extremely thirsty, and confused as to why I was in Hell of all places.

I began to walk through Hell trying to find a way out. I eventually stumbled upon Death himself, The Grim Reaper. I asked him, "Where is Jesus" and he laughed in my face and said, "You're in Hell, Jesus is not here!" At that moment I woke up like I said terrified and sweat pouring down my entire body like I had just gotten out of the shower and had not dried off yet. My bed was soaked from all the sweat that had poured off of my body. I didn't know what the heck just happened all I know was I was in Hell, I was no longer in Hell, and I never wanted to go back to Hell ever again!

I also know Hell is real because of the Demons that controlled my life regarding the struggles I faced with my mental health as well as the struggles I faced with self harming, drugs and alcohol. There's another quote that goes, "When Darkness Is All You Know, You Begin To Fear The Light" but there is also another quote I'd like to point out that goes, "Even In Darkness, There Is Light!" When things keep happening in your life to negatively effect your life it's so easy to get so discouraged that you fear things actually getting any better. But on the same note we have to remember that without negativity there is no reason for positivity to exist. If everything was sunshine and rainbows all the time there would be no need for God or for the free gift that Jesus made possible for us to have. If Adam and Even obeyed God and never disobeyed God sure there would be no sin in the world but then Jesus would never have had to be born and crucified giving us a place in Heaven alongside him and God the Father.

Another argument that people throw around when

it comes to God and Christianity as a whole is, "If God loves us so much why would he allow pain and suffering, why would he allow his people to get things like cancer, why would he allow good people and or young people to be murdered in cold blood?" The answer is simple, Trust is key! When you became old enough if you did so after cellphones became a thing, You're parents didn't just give you a cellphone one day, No they gave you a cellphone when they knew you could be trusted with a cellphone. You don't tell someone you can't trust one of your deepest darkest secrets do you? God allows bad things to happen in the world he created to see how we react and if we chose to trust in him or condemn him. As far as things like cancer I love telling people who question that, "God gives his fiercest battles to his strongest soldiers because he knows that person has the ability to over come that obstacle and become a warrior!"

When you allow God to place obstacles in your life and you chose to trust in him instead of condemn him. He not only rewards you but he gives you one heck of a story to tell every time. How do I know this, because this entire book is nothing but obstacles God has placed in my life. And how I chose to trust in him and now here I am writing my story for you to read and for you to see that God has given me one heck of a story to tell. That has victory after victory in it all because I chose to trust in him and turn to him in even the darkest of times to seek comfort and guidance in him so that I could make it to where I am today with this amazing story to tell. I wouldn't go back and redo a single moment of my life, this story has made me who I am today and has gotten me to where I am today.

My favorite verse in the entire bible is Philippians 3:12-14, " I don't mean to say that I have already achieved these things or that I have already reached perfection. But I press on to possess that perfection for which Christ Jesus first possessed me. No, dear brothers and sisters, I have not achieved it, but I focus on this one thing: Forgetting the past and looking forward to what lies ahead. I press on to reach the end of the race and receive the heavenly prize for which God, through Christ Jesus, is calling us." That verse just speaks to me so loudly very time I hear it. To know that no one is perfect but that perfection is the goal as Christ Jesus was and is perfection that one day we be exactly like him, is just so reassuring.

One of my favorite worship songs is Cornerstone by Hillsong. My favorite part is the chorus where it says, "Christ alone, Cornerstone, The weak made strong in the Saviors love, Through the storm, He is Lord, Lord of all." Every time I hear that or sing that portion of the song a tingle always runs down my spine and I can just feel the presence of the Holy Spirit flowing through me. I love music from Hillsong, another song by them I really enjoy is "Take It All" it goes, "Jesus we're living for your name, We'll never be ashamed of you, All praise and all we are today, Take, Take, Take it all, Take, Take, Take it all." That song is a little more upbeat so if you're into more contemporary music it probably won't be your cup of tea. But it's good song none the less with a powerful message to it.

Skillet is definitely my all time favorite Christian band ever. I previously mention in my chapter about my mental health how I was one of ninety one people chosen to have their picture featured in the fan lyric video for Sick Of It by Skillet back in 2013 but I have another memory of Skillet that is way better. Each year there is a Christian music festival known as Winter Jam, Usually when it comes to my area it comes to Reading, Pennsylvania. I never went because I always thought it was for girls as when I was in youth group that was an activity the girls did every year and it was only for the girls of the youth group. My mom told me it wasn't for just girls that anyone could go to Winter Jam and I saw that last year, 2022, Skillet was the headlining band. I told my mom I wanted to go with her and she told me that would be awesome but I had to get the Jam Nation package as that's what everyone in the group she was going with was getting. Now the Jam Nation package gave you early access into the even as well as front stage seating.

We arrived at the venue and found the line we were to be in and we could even see the buses for some of the bands. As we waited and waited for the doors to open we talked with other people in line and and took turns saving our spot in line so each other could go to the bathroom or get food, etc. At one point we were in line and my friend said, "Look over there its Korey Cooper and Jen Ledger." I thought he was pulling my leg but he was serious. We went over and Jen kept walking and Korey stopped and my buddy was able to get a picture with her but when I asked she said she really had to get going so I didn't put up a fuss. I told my friend how lucky he was and how jealous I was of him for getting a picture with Korey freakin' Cooper the guitarist from Skillet.

We ended up finding seats four rows from the front of the stage and right next to the catwalk of the stage. I was so stoked that we had great seats cause I knew if I really wanted to I'd be able to reach out and touch the people on stage but didn't for fear the security would get after me. There were some other awesome bands there other then Skillet like I Am They, Newsboys, Colon Dixon and KB. Since we got the Jam Nation package and got early access into the show we got to see the Pre Jam which was up and coming artists. One that I really liked was Abby Robertson she even played a song that she hadn't yet released at the time but as of writing this book she just released it a few weeks ago called, Unstoppable, That song really spoke to me as it really hit home with everything I struggled with in my past. The chorus goes,

"I'm unstoppable, Cause my God's unstoppable and, All things are possible, Cause I know where my help comes from, I got a hope unshakable, And a faith unbreakable yeah, All things are possible, Cause my God is unstoppable." The song is basically about when you think something isn't possible just remember that nothing is impossible with God.

During the intermission time I went out to the merchandise area and I met Abby Robertson and told her I really loved her performance and I got my picture taken with her. After that I went to the Skillet table, of course, and I purchased John Coopers book, "Awake & Alive To Truth", Great book by the way a true must read. I also go a copy of their new CD Dominion as well as a completely autographed by every member in the band photo that I guarded with my absolute life for the rest of the night.

Abby Robertson and I at Winter Jam 2023 in Reading, PA.

After the intermission was over we went back to our seats and when it was time for Skillet to take the stage I was READY. The lights went out and Skillet took the stage and I as well as everyone else in the arena went completely mental. I took so many pictures and videos of Skillet it was crazy.

We were so close you could feel the pyro cooking our skin but I didn't care, it was SKILLET! They delivered banger after banger after banger and we in the crowd rocked hard and hard and harder. At one point John Cooper the lead singer came out on the catwalk with a copy of his book in his hand continuing to sing and he stopped right in front of me and my friend. My friend reached his hand out looking for a high five from John but instead John put the book into my friends hand. I told him to open the cover that I bet it was autographed, my friend opened the book and sure enough it had John Coopers autograph in it. I tried to convince him to trade me his copy of the book for my copy I purchased at the merchandise stand and he said, "Absolutely not!"

A few songs later John Cooper. Jen Ledger and Korey Cooper came out on the catwalk and I put my hand out and Jen Ledger gave me a high five. I went CRAZY, I couldn't believe one of the best female drummer in the entire world just gave me a high five. It was truly the greatest night of my life. By the time the show was over my voice was completely shot from all the yelling I did. And I was absolutely drenched in

Skillet preforming at Winter Jam 2022 in Reading, PA.

sweat from all the jumping around I had done as well as from the heat from the pyro. But was it worth it, absolutely, would I do it again, of course.

And I did do it again as a little over a year later and a few months ago from writing this book I went to see Skillet perform again at the same venue on this time it was with Saint Asonia and Theory Of A Deadman as part of the Resurrection Rock Tour. This time however I had to settle for being a bit further back as my friends didn't want to go to close to the stage and it truly was a packed house and one of those things were you get in where you fit in. I had never seen Saint Asonia before nor had I ever heard of them before and I never saw Theory Of A Deadman before but I've definitely heard about them. Saint Asonia went on first and put up one heck of an opening act. Then Skillet took the stage and of course it was absolutely amazing. They even debuted their song Finish Line and even had the singer from Saint Asonia help them sing it as in the song he is actually a featured artist.

After Skillet had finished their performance my friends and I decided we didn't really care to see Theory Of A Deadman and decided to head out. Before heading out though we stopped at the merchandise table which was absolutely swamped with people. They were actually running two or three lines because there was so many people in line. I bought a tour t-shirt and settled with just that as my money was running tight at this point. Though we didn't stay for Theory Of A Deadman the show was an absolute banger. Skillet is definitely one of my all time favorite bands to see live.

Words can absolutely not begin to describe just how much Skillet and their music have impacted my life. They opened my eyes to the fact that just because I failed college that doesn't mean I'm a failure. Their music has helped me see that you are not defined by your past. And of course John Cooper's book, "Awake & Alive To Truth" definitely helped inspire my personal life to live my life better and better with each passing day for Christ. I wish I could meet each and every member of Skillet and let them know the impact that they've had on my life. Even Jen Ledger and her band Ledger, that music has helped me through some tough times in life especially with my mental health.

<u>*Chapter 10*</u>

SOBRIETY, RECOVERY & RELAPSE

"Behold, I will bring to it health and healing,
and I will heal them; and I will reveal to them
an abundance of peace and truth."
- Jeremiah 33:6

I feel like when you see the words sobriety, recovery and relapse there is a lot of negativity surrounding those words. You say I'm this many years sober and people automatically assume you were this raging alcoholic who would wet their cheerios in the morning with beer. When you say you're in recovery people atomically assume you must have been a crack head or a meth addict. And when you say you relapsed people focus on the fact that means you failed to stay clean or sober or whatever when that's just not always the case. Also people who are trying to get sober or clean from drugs and alcohol there's just so many things in this world to cause them to fail and it's honestly sad. And then there is the mental health aspect of sobriety and recovery.

I watch this women on YouTube who says, "We recovery loudly, so those behind us don't have to suffer in silence." I think that is an absolutely amazing quote as it give encouragement for people with a story to share they're story in hopes that it might encourage and or help those still struggling to find the courage and will to become sober or clean themselves. Addiction is a true demon and it's so sad to see people struggle with addiction and feel helpless and hopeless. Just like mental health there are resources you can go to in order to get help. And more importantly there are people who care about you and love you and want to see you become sober and clean and free of those demons hold you down, keeping you prisoner to whatever you weapons of choice are be it alcohol, weed, heroin, meth, etc. And remember recovery is possible and your life matters.

Now lets get to me and my story regarding sobriety, recovery and relapse. Put your seat belts on because it's about to be a bumpy road. I quite smoking cigarettes shortly after I started when I was eighteen because like I stated before I just could afford the habit. I stopped smoking marijuana and K2 around the same time back in 2013 after my friend Adam had been arrested for murdering Ashley. I mention in the chapter about my mental health how I sought help for self harming and was required to go through an Intensive Outpatient Program which I attended for five months before being released. I sought help in March of 2019 and that was the last time I self harmed.

In November of 2021 my great grandma on my mother's side of the family was not doing so well and was admitted to the hospital. My grandma told me if I wanted to visit my great grandma in the hospital I better do it sooner rather then later. My sister and I went in to visit that night and then the next day I told my mom if she wanted to see great grandma she better do it soon as they're not giving her long as far as time left to be alive. My mom and I went in and my great grandma's one step daughter was there as she was my great grandma's power of attorney. She had asked my mother and I if we were going to be there long because she wanted to go back to her hotel room and shower quickly and change into some fresh clothing, My mom and I told her that we would stay as long as we needed to and told her not to rush. She thanked us and went on her way.

Shortly after she left my great grandma's vitals began to decrease, The bell on her vital machine had started to ping and my mom just looked over at me as the doctor and nurses came running into the room. My mom asked me if great grandma was in the process of passing and I said, "I believe so." The doctor had confirmed that my great grandma was indeed in her final moments and asked the whereabouts of the power of attorney. We told him she had just left to go back to her hotel and shower and change. The doctor asked if we were family and my mom said yes identifying her as one of the grandchildren on my great grandma and me as one of the great grandchildren of my great grandma. The doctor had told us the we could take all the time we needed with my great grandma even after she passes and that if we needed anything at all to let someone know.

He then along with all the nurses exited the room and pulled the privacy curtain after explaining to us that we would hear my great grandma making a few noises and moans and groans for a little but that was basically just oxygen leaving her body. My mom had told me she was going to call some family and let them know that great grandma had passed and had asked me to call my grandma. I went out in the hallway called my grandma and as soon as I began to speak I broke down into tears. My grandma told me to breath and speak when I was ready to. I told her, "She's gone, Great Grandma is gone!" My grandma knew I meant my great grandma had passed and thanked me for relaying the message to her and told me to try and calm down.

After some time my mom and I had decided to go home. My mom dropped me off at my house and then headed to her house. This is when things would go downhill for me. I immediately began drinking alcohol after a few drinks I got out a razor blade and began cutting my arm. For the first time in two years and eight months I had self harmed causing me to relapse in my self harm recovery. It wasn't that my great grandma had passed away that caused me to self harm but it was the fact I literally watched as it happened.

I watched as her heart rate dropped lower and lower until bell on the machine started going off signaling something was wrong, I watched as my great grandma took her final breaths, I heard my great grandma taking her final breaths, I heard the moans and the groan's of her final moments alive, and I have been there the moment she passed away. That's enough to mess up even the strongest person mentally. Seeing all that and hearing all that had broke me mentally. And in that moment of weakness I had turned to and old friend, the blade, for comfort and used alcohol to cover up the pain I felt inside in that moment. When I realized what I had done and that I had indeed relapsed in my self harm recovery and just threw away two years and eight months of recovery I immediately felt guilt and shame. And no amount of alcohol was going to be able to cover up the amount of guilt and shame that I had felt in that moment.

I knew that it was official, I was back to square on in my recovery as far as self harm. Six months later in May of 2022 I decided that I was going to clean my life up so I didn't relapse again. I stopped drinking alcohol all together, I stopped chewing tobacco all together and I promised myself I'd never self harm again no matter how hard things get. In May of this year, 2023, I celebrated my one year anniversary of being sober and clean from any and all drugs and alcohol. In November of this year, 2023,

I will celebrate two years in recovery from self harm since my relapse and July 2024 I will officially be back to where I was in my recovery from self harm when I previously relapsed. Two years and eight months in recovery is the longest I've ever gone in recovery from self harm.

Nothing and no one is going to stop me from getting to that two years and three month mark and then I will go two years and eight months more after that and I will continue to stay strong and stay in recovery for the rest of my life. I promise myself as well as everyone reading this book that I will never again relapse in my self harm recovery journey ever again. I can confidently say that my mental illness no longer has dominion over me but that I have dominion over my mental illness. I am stronger then I was before, I am a warrior. Like the Ledger song Warrior says, "Never give up, Never back down, I will die before I bow!" I have so much to look forward to and so many reason to stay strong. Plus I know that there are a ton of people who will be in line ready to put a shoe where the sun don't shine if I ever relapse again.

I've always been a major advocate for mental health awareness and suicide awareness. That's one of the big reasons I decided to go through the programs offered by iPrevail Health and become a Peer To Peer Councilor and then a Mentor. It's still hard for me to this day to listen to Ghost by Bad Flower and not feel guilt and shame from the times I use to play that song while self harming. When it comes on I can listen to it and be fine, I don't think about self harming anymore I just feel negative emotions stemming from my decisions of the past. I will forever be an advocate for mental health awareness and suicide awareness as I truly believe they are two issues that don't receive enough attention especially these days. Mental Health is running wild these days and it effects more and more people day after day.

I even enjoy doing things to bring awareness to the issues of mental health and suicide. A few of my favorite things to do through out the year is to participate in The Heart Project and To Write Love On Her Arms Day. The Heart Project is July 10th-15th each and every year. You draw hearts on your arm in different colors that apply to you, each colored heart represents a different mental illness or aspect of mental illness such as Anxiety, Depression, OCD, Self Harm, etc. To Write Love On Her Arms Day also known as Suicide Prevention Day is September 10th and you are to write the word LOVE on your arm and go about your day with LOVE written on your arm as a way to raise awareness to the growing rate of suicide and how suicide can be prevented. More about The Heart Project can be found on Facebook just search for The Heart Project or #TheHeartProject and more about To Write Love On Her Arms Day can be found at www.TWLOHA.com.

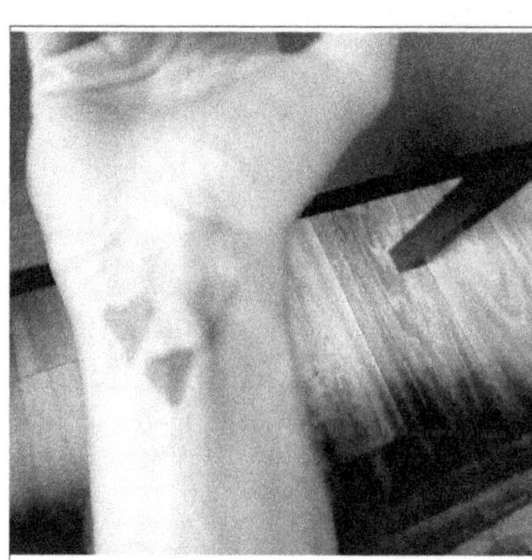

My participation in The Heart Project 2023.

It's not just adults being effected either, more and more children are being effected by mental health issues with each passing day. According to the Substance Abuse and Mental Health Services Administration as on April 2023, One in five adult Americans experienced a mental health condition in any given year. One in six young people have experienced a major depressive episode. One in twenty Americans have lived with a serious mental illness, such as schizophrenia, bipolar disorder, or major depression. According to the World Health Organization three hundred and fifty million people worldwide suffer from depression. Each year an estimated eight hundred thousand people take their own lives which is twice the number of people who die from malaria.

Suicide is the second highest cause of death among people age fifteen to twenty nine years of age. Suicide percentages are especially high among girls and young women. Those are just some of the facts surrounding Mental Illness and Suicide. As someone who's been suicidal in the past as well as someone who has lost loved one's to suicide I can tell you neither end of the stick feels good. I've mentioned a few quotes so far in this book and I'd like to reference one more, "Suicide is a permanent solution to temporary problems!" People commit suicide most times because they feel like it's the only way to get rid of the pain and or negative emotions they are experiencing.

I mentioned the song Monsters by Shinedown in the chapter about my struggles with my mental health. The chorus of that song goes, "Cause my monster are real, and they're trained how to kill, There's no comin' back and they just laugh at how I feel, And these monster can fly, And they'll never say die, And there's no goin' back if I get trapped I'll never heal, Yeah, My monsters are real." My monsters where my issues with my mental health and they were fueled by drugs and alcohol, alcohol especially. Whenever I drank especially in times of hurt or pain in my life I would always think about self harming. And that is how I knew that alcohol definitely needed to be extinguished from my life. That was the motivation and the thing that gave me the determination to quit drinking alcohol.

There's a verse in the Shinedown song Monsters that goes, "Leave your weapon on the table, Wrapped in burlap barely able, Call a doctor say your prayers, Chose a God you think is fair." That is exactly how I overcame my monsters or demons if you will of self harm, I laid down the razor blade aka my weapon, put it away out of sight out of mind, sought help from a doctor and believed that God would guide me and strengthen me to find victory over my monsters or demons. Another think I'm very thankful for is that I don't seem to have a very addictive personality. For most people when they decided to quit something like drugs or alcohol they have to go to rehab or specific classes but for me I seem to be able to tell myself I'm going to quit doing something and quit doing that thing cold turkey. For most people it can get quit expensive for them to quit they're bad habits as therapy and rehab are not cheap even with health insurance.

The COVID-19 Pandemic was a hard time for everyone. If you were lucky like me and were able to have your job deemed essential and you an essential worker you got to continue to work through the pandemic. During that time and still as of writing this book I work at a nursing home and rehabilitation center, for privacy reasons I'm not going to give the name of the facility nor the company that operates the facility but I will say that during the COVID-19 pandemic things got dark fast. A good majority of the residents had contracted the virus and a good majority of the residents who contracted the virus had sadly passes away, not all due to the virus but of complications there of. Things got so bad that the company had offered us grief counseling at one point in time due to how many residents we lost. The local newspaper was even writing articles about the facility and how terrible it was and the painting the works to sound like heartless monsters who just didn't care.

That was the farthest thing from the truth as many tears were shed as resident after resident had passed away during that time. This time was especially hard for me mentally as when I'm at work I enjoy talking with and joking around with the residents. I remember this two residents who were married and were both in the COVID wing of the facility due to contracting COVID but were in separate rooms that I very much enjoyed talking with and joking around with even prior to the COVID pandemic. The man would always come to his wife's room and spend all day in her room with her and even feed her meals to her prior to COVID. During COVID the residents obviously weren't allowed out of their rooms as a measure to keep the virus contained and controlled. Since the man could no longer visit with his wife he would write her love letters every day and even occasionally draw her a picture.

When I would come to his room to clean his room he would give me the the letter he wrote and or the picture he drew for his wife and ask me to give them to his wife when I got to cleaning her room. So everyday I would take this mans love letter and or drawing and give them to his wife when I got to her room. The man had passed during the pandemic but his wife is still with us today. She still tells me how much it meant to her to have me bring her those letters and drawings from her husband during the pandemic and how thankful she is for me being kind enough to do that for him. I didn't even do that for them to be a "kind" person, I did it because I knew it was something so small that meant the entire world to the both of them and would make a time that was so miserable for most people less miserable for the two of them.

Things like this was also the reason that when I was offered grief counseling as a result of all the residents who had passed during that time, I respectfully declined it. I try to go to work each and every day, even before and after the pandemic reminding myself that I work in an environment that mostly services those who are at the end of the road when it comes to their lives. I try to remember that I could talk to a resident on any given day and the next day they could be gone as no one is immune to death. I love my job and I enjoy my job and honestly I have no intentions of leaving this job any time soon. Heck I can even go to work feeling anxious or depressed or just feeling down in the dumps and residents who know me well will ask me what's wrong and offer to talk to me and brighten up my day each and every time. I have so many memories from my job that I wouldn't trade for the world.

If you or a loved one is struggling with drugs or alcohol or any addiction for that matter please get help. And if you or a loved one are struggling mentally remember your life matters, there are people who care and love you, and please seek help. If you or a loved one are feeling suicidal or having suicidal thoughts or tendencies please seek help immediately. You may think that no one cares or that no one will miss you but I promise there is someone who cares about you enough to see you get help. Your stronger then your Monsters, Your demons don't have to control you, You can control your life!

If you or someone you love is in crisis contact the Suicide Prevention Lifeline at 1-800-273-TALK (8255), or dial 911 in the case of an emergency!

If you or someone you love is struggling with their mental health or substance abuse contact the Substance Abuse and Mental Health Services Administration at 1-800-662-HELP (4357), or dial 911 in case of an emergency!

Chapter 11

BECOMING A CHRISTIAN

"Believe on the Lord Jesus Christ,
and you shall be saved!"
- Acts 16:31

Remember how in the chapter when I talked about how Christ Jesus came to this earth and lived life as a mortal man and eventually would be crucified and later raise from the dead and ascend into Heaven to reside with God The Father and that because of that we can have the free gift of eternal life through Christ Jesus by asking him into your heart to be the Lord and Savior of your life? Right now we are going to talk more about that and then I will tell you how you can do all that and then provide you with a prayer that you can pray to obtain that free gift that Christ Jesus offers to everyone who believes, so that you can have your permanent place in Heaven secured and your name written in the Lambs Book Of Life! Now I know what your thinking, "If it's a free gift why do I need to do anything in order to get it?" Well because as I stated in the chapter about Christ's life he wants you to make the decision to give your life to him. He wants you to trust in him enough to allow him to reside within your heart and drive the bus when it comes to your life. Now lets dive into the steps necessary when it comes to Salvation through Christ Jesus our Lord.

The first step is to realize and to admit that you are in fact a sinner. Like Adam and Eve sinned against God in the Garden of Eden causing sin to enter the world, We are effected by their decision even to this day. The next step is to understand and believe that God sent his son Jesus to this earth to be crucified on the cross and in his crucifixion bared the sins of the world upon him and he bled and died on that cross so that we could be forgiven of our sins. Next we need to understand and realize that Jesus then rose from the grave three days later and would eventually go to Heaven to prepare a place for all who give their lives to him through salvation. Once you understand and believe those things you must pray and repent of your sins and then ask Jesus to come into your heart and cleanse you over your sins and be the Lord of your life. After you cover those things in prayer, GREAT NEWS, You are officially what Christians refer to as saved and you now posses that free gift which Christ Jesus made possible through his death, burial, and resurrection.

Your not done there though, The first step in your journey as a born again Christian is to identify with Jesus Christ in his burial and resurrection through what is called water baptism or simply referred to as baptism. This is don't by someone ordained to do so, usual the pastor of a church. You and the person baptizing you will enter a body of water deep enough for you to be completely submerged and the person performing the baptism will ask you to profess that you are indeed a Christian and have asked the Lord to come into your life. They will then tell you that based upon your admission of being a Christian and that you have already invited the Lord into your life, They baptize you in the name of The Father, The Son and the Holy Spirit as they submerge you under the water and bring you back up again. After they bring you up out of the water you officially have identified with Christ in his burial and resurrection and have now officially been baptized and washed clean of all your inequities. But the next part of your journey is the part that is the hardest and that people around you and in your life with notice the most.

Now it is time for you to prove that everything you just did was not for show or because you know it's the right thing to do, or simply for some ritual. But rather because you truly and honestly believe in everything Christ gave so that you could be free and that you are no longer a slave to the sins of your past but a new creation, born again through Christ Jesus. That he dwells inside of you and that one day you will go to Heaven to be with Christ Jesus and God The Father in eternity. This can only be done by living your daily life day after day reflecting your decision to allow Christ into your life by making sure the words of your mouth and the actions of your heart reflect that of Christ Jesus. The world will still judge you based upon your actions, but God will judge you based on the context of your heart. Now I will give you an example of a prayer you can pray to repent of your sins and to invite the Lord into your heart and into your life so that you may take the first step into becoming a Christian!

"Lord,
I know that I'm a sinner. I know that I've done things in my life that aren't pleasing to you. I'd like for you to forgive me of my sins, I believe and boldly proclaim that you died on the cross and rose again so that I could be free. I ask that right now you come into my heart and be the Lord of my life. That I may be a new creation in and through you, Christ Jesus my Lord.
In Your Holy and Precious Name,
Amen!"

If you prayed that simple prayer or one similar to it you have been what it's called "born again." You are a new creation in Christ Jesus our Lord. You now have a permanent place in Heaven as a citizen. It says in the bible that God is preparing a place for you, and that in Heaven there are many mansions, and you are the proud new owner of a mansion in Heaven. If you said that simple prayer I want you to tell someone you love and care about that you made the decision to give your life to Christ. Trust me it feels oh so good to share the news with others.

I also encourage you to find yourself a church to attend. And not just any church but one where you feel the presence of God Almighty reigning through it. It's not so much about the building itself as that isn't the church but rather the people inside the building that are considered the church. A good place of worship is a vital part to a healthy relationship with Christ. Remember earlier how I said that Jesus should be your Savior and not your religion? Well now is the time to make that more true then ever.

If you live your life with Jesus being your religion, your going to see things like prayer and going to church as nothing more then a ritual or the right thing to do. If Jesus is your Savior and you honestly and truly believe that things like prayer become a way of intimately communicating with God. Going to church seems less of a chore and more of a place you can gather with fellow believers in Christ and celebrate your relationship with him through praise and worship with your fellow believers. Going to church also gives you the opportunity to hear the word of God preached to you by one of his gifted messengers. Getting to know people within your church of choice is great as well because it gives you people who can help you stay accountable in your relationship with Christ. Going to church and making friends with others in the congregation also gives you positive influences in your life as well as friendships that you know will impact you positively.

Another important aspect of your relationship with Christ is going to be staying grounded within his word. If you read your Bible and you believe what it says to be true, you can become a true warrior for Christ when it comes to combating the evil of the enemy Satan. If you not only read your Bible but you really study what it says and memorize what it says you can reference and use what it says in your day to day life in order to stay devoted and dedicated to Christ Jesus. A good way to study the Bible is to make daily devotions a part of your daily life. This is where you devote some time each day to reading and studying the Bible and figuring out how you can apply what you read to your life so that you may be stronger in you walk with God. Prayer is a good way to kick off and to end your time of daily devotion to the Lord as well.

Also now that you are officially a Christian remember that the next important decision for you to make is to identify yourself with Christ in his burial and resurrection through being baptized in water. This is also why finding a church to ground yourself into is a good idea after accepting Christ into your life as many church offer the chance to be baptized at least once a year if not multiple times a year. I had the privilege of being baptized when I was ten and I even had the honor and the privilege of aiding my disabled brother into the baptismal at our church and helping him out of the baptismal after he had been baptized. This was a proud moment for me as he not only got baptized on his birthday that year which happens to fall every year on Halloween, one of the most evil and satanic holidays of the year. But he is also a former Satanist who has since given his life to Christ and uses his disabilities to be an inspiration to others. He is literally most times the first person at the alter at church and the last person to leave the alter.

After you get baptized you can live your life in a manor that is pleasing to God day after day. You've done all you need to do in order to align yourself with Christ. You now officially, if your living your life in a way that pleases Christ and your not being influenced by sin and repenting of any sins you may commit along the way, have made Jesus your Savior and not your religion. Things will not be easy, and definitely won't be a piece of cake to stay on the straight and narrow as the enemy come to kill, steal and destroy especially those who have aligned themselves with Christ. The Devil wants you to fall and become discouraged. It's his mission to drive you as far away from Christ as possible and to keep you from living a life that is pleasing to God.

During the COVID-19 Pandemic the lead singer of Hawk Nelson had questioned what kind of God would allow such a virus to run as wild through the entire world as the COVID-19 virus killing as many people as it had up to that point. He then proclaimed that for that reason he no longer believed in God and denounced his faith in God. This is exactly what the enemy wants to see in Christians. He wants to see them doubt God and question God to the point they no longer believe and turn away from God. If the enemy can cause a person like the lead singer of a Christian band like Hawk Nelson to denounce God, Think about how effortless it would be for him to do the same to you or I if we are not grounded in our relationship with Christ. It's definitely something to spend some serious time thinking about.

Like I said back in the chapter where I focus on Christ Jesus and his life I stated how God allows bad things to happen as a way to see just how much we trust him or if we will flee from him or even condemn him. In many religions if you do not bow or you do not worship the God of that religion the right way, The God of that religion will have you thrown in jail or worst put to death. That is what makes Christ Jesus different from all other Gods, He doesn't do things out of vengeance or malice, He doesn't seek to gain revenge on those who have done him wrong. The God of The Bible only does things out of love which if you've been paying attention to the verses after the title of each chapter I referenced in my chapter about my parents divorce a verse defining love, 1 Corinthians 13:4-7. It goes, "Love is patient, Love is kind, It does not envy, It does not boast, It is not proud. It does not dishonor others, it is not self-seeking, it is not easily angered, and it keeps no record of wrongs." That is what the God of The Bible is all about.

In this day and age it's harder then ever to be a Christian as Christianity is under attack by the enemy via many different political assaults. Things have gotten so bad that fewer and fewer young people are attending church. In fact only twenty eight percent of Generation Z Americans say they are committed to attending religious services of any kind at least once a month. Fourteen percent identify as Atheist, meaning they believe there is no God, or Agnostic, meaning they believe that nothing is or can be know regarding God. And that is all results of a survey done back in December 2022 by The Walton Family Foundation and Murmuration in conjunction with SocialSphere. I don't know about you but that is honestly and truly so heart crushing to me.

Generation Z would rather believe there is no God or that we don't know enough about God to say weather or not he exists and that he is the God of The Bible over believing there is a God and putting their trust and faith in him so that they may have eternal life in Heaven and completely obliterate any possibility of them burning for all eternity in the fiery pits of Hell. When I went to school we started each day by reciting the Pledge Of Allegiance where one line of it was, "One nation under God" but that has since been taken out of schools. Even when I was in school they would tell you that if you felt uncomfortable saying that part of the pledge you could just simply not say that part when we got to that part of the pledge. I've even had people of generations before mine tell me about how prayer use to be a part of the school day but was eventually taken out of the schools. Our nations motto still we remains, "In God We Trust" which at this point is somewhat surprising to me that we haven't changed that to. In a nation that was founded on Christian morals and beliefs, not entirely but partially none the less we have managed to almost completely take God out of our nation who still claims, "In God We Trust!"

This next part isn't going to sit well with many people and may even rustle a few feathers but I truly feel it's something God wants me to touch upon. God has been removed from our school system and had been replaced with programming our children and our youth with corrupt and tyrannical theories. Theories such as, "If you're White, You're the problem" or "You can be whatever you want to be even if it means believing you have a tail and animal ears and communicate via animal noises while wearing a collar and a leash, going to the bathroom in a liter box." We are even telling these young impressionable, easily influenced children and youth that there are multiple gender they can chose from, not just male or female." Explain to me though why when these young children and youth seek gender reassignment surgeries they are only given two options, Male To Female or Female To Male, no other options, no Male To Toaster or Female To Pony. You can't be a Christian and honestly believe there is more then Male or Female genders and that you are pronounced as one or the other at the time of your birth based upon your genitalia at that time.

It doesn't mean though that when you see someone who believes this way that you should make fun of them or condemn them to Hell. No the Christian and Like Christ thing to do would be to treat them with the love of Christ and at least attempt to share the gospel with them in hopes that through your kindness and lack of persecution upon them that they may see the light and come to the decision to change their ways and give their life to Christ as well. There's a verse in the Bible that says, "Love your neighbor as yourself" or in simpler terms, "Treat others the way you want to be treated." In fact it's not just a verse in the Bible but it is also one of the Ten Commandments. When The Bible refers to your neighbor it's not just talking about the person who lives next to you, but to everyone you see and come in contact with through out your day and even your life. That is what the Bible means when it says to Love your neighbor, It means to love EVERYONE!

It also says in the Bible that we are to hate the sin not the sinner meaning we should never hate another human being no matter how different they may be or what lifestyle they choose to live. It also says in the Bible that if you have hate towards your fellow man that in your heart you have already committed murder. God hates no one and beings we are created in his image we should have hate for no one as well. Even Satan, God had at one point had love for Satan as he was actually an angel in Heaven at one point. God cast Satan down to hell along with all his followers not because he hated Satan but because Satan's britches got a little to big for him in Heaven and went against God.

I know what it's like to be judged based upon your appearance. I have multiple tattoo's and multiple piercings and if I had a penny for every time I got a dirty look when mentioning I'm a Christian or someone's told me they didn't expect me to be as serious about my relationship with Christ as I am because of my tattoo's and or piercings I'd be rich. I even have had people assume I must be a criminal because I have tattoo's and or piercings. Some have admitted to me they doubted my seriousness in my walk with Christ and have been shocked at just how serious I actually am about my relationship with Christ.

This just goes to show the age old quote, "Don't judge a book by it's cover" to be extremely true.

I'm so serious about my relationship with Christ that I even participated and completed a discipleship program through Emotionally Health. I completed the Spirituality course and plan on taking part in the Relationships course in September 2023. I was offered the opportunity by Hillsong Church in New York, NY to take part in the courses online via Zoom meetings. Once I complete this next course I will be able to take part in the courses in the future as whats called a Table Leader meaning I will be given a group of participants to lead through the course. Discipleship is important to your relationship with Christ as it is you doing the Lords work here on earth.

I remember the first time I had shared my testimony. It was a bit scary because I wasn't sure if people were going to judge me or think differently of my afterward, but in the end I was glad I did. It was when I attended Grace Fellowship Church of Ephrata, I was in my early to mid twenties and the Pastor had everyone who felt comfortable doing so write out their testimony and put it into a jar. Each Sunday he picked two or three names from the jar and gave them the opportunity to share their testimony. One Sunday he pulled my name and I accepted the chance to share my testimony with the church. After I had got done sharing after the service I had so many people telling me how inspirational my testimony was. Ever since that say I have been proud of my testimony and you should be as well, If you get the chance to share your testimony please do I promise you won't regret it!

Your testimony is your story and it is unique to you. There will never be a testimony like yours ever in the history of humanity. Their may be ones that sound similar to yours or that you may be able to relate with, but testimonies are never duplicated. They are your story from death to life in Jesus Christ our Lord. Take pride in your story even if it has not so great details in it. Just look at my story and the horrible things I have done yet I don't regret them because without them my story wouldn't be as powerful as it is.

I challenge you to if you have not done so already, write your own testimony. Write it on paper and keep it in your lock box or whatever, type it out and keep it on your computer or laptop, Heck here's one I bet you never heard before. Try typing up your testimony as a note of your phone that way you have an on-the-go version of your testimony that you can carry around in your pocket. That way when you come across someone who is a perfect opportunity to share your testimony with you can pull your phone out, open that note and begin sharing your story given to you by God to display the work he's done in your through him. You never know when the Lord will give you the opportunity to witness to a non-believer so why not be prepared at all times. And who knows by doing so you may just lead an unsaved person to the Lord and add to the ever growing citizenship of Heaven.

<u>*LIVING FEARLESSLY*</u>

Essentially everything you just read in this book was a very detailed version of my testimony as a Christian. As you can see I wasn't kidding when I said that Christ has been part of my life since a young age. And because of that a life in Christ is really all I know. As you can also see I tried living my life my way and all it got me was rides in the back of a police car, abuse of numerous substances, and a lot of failure through out my life. Didn't really work out so well for me, huh? So I had to call in the big guns to get things right!

Once I made the decision to stop living life on my own terms and letting others influence me and my life, life got exponentially better. Nearly ever aspect of my life I began to see major improvements. I began doing daily devotionals every day, I decided to read through the entire Bible in a year, I began praying daily. The more and more time out of my day I devoted to God the more and more I began to see him moving in life and continuing to mold me and make me into the man he planned for me to be. I also began to trust and have more faith in him then I ever have before. I even found my attention in church and participation in church to have increased greatly.

My mental health has also gotten so much better since giving God full control over my life. I'm not nearly as anxious as I use to be, I no longer have any desire to self harm, when I do worry and begin to stress, a simple prayer easily calms me down. I have even been able to offer better advice to others who struggle with mental health issues. I am so happy to have control over this aspect of my life and definitely owe it all to Jesus. And trust me I will never go back to how I use to be when it comes to my mental health. It's not an option now, a week from now, a month from now, not ever!

I mentioned quite a few songs and lyrics within this book so why not mention one more before I call this book finished. There's a song called Amazing Grace by Chris Tomlin and the second verse is my favorite ever. It says, "My chains are gone I've been set free. My God my Savior has ransomed me, And like a floor his mercy reigns. Unending love, Amazing Grace." These lyrics have never been so true, especially in my life.

I've definitely had my fair share of chains in my life before I let Christ run my life. And it was only when I let Christ take the reigns of my life that I saw the cracks in those chains begin to form and those chains eventually break apart setting me free. What he did on the cross has made it so I can live the life I have today without any worry of fear. Without the price Christ paid on the cross my life today wouldn't be the same, I'm quite positive of that. And it's only because of his mercy and his grace that my past doesn't define who I am today. Now I end this book saying because of Christ and his impact on my life I am, FEARLESS OVER FAILURE!

ABOUT THE AUTHOR

Jaime Moyer is an ENFJ personality type to the core known best for his extreme levels of energy. Jaime enjoys being outdoors taking walks through nature and cruising around on his 50cc gas powered scooter or on one of his multiple skateboards. He love to be surrounded by family and friends whenever possible. Jaime also goes by the name Axl Fox online and in his career as a Referee in the Professional Wrestling Industry where he has met many people who have inspired him to join the industry from watching them such as Thunder Rosa, Sabu, Sandman, and Daffney to name a few. Jaime's hobbies include playing video games on his PlayStation 4, Skateboarding in the streets as well as local skate parks and Drawing via a verity of different mediums such as felt tip marker, colored pencil, and acrylic paint and has even won various ribbons at the local fairs for his drawings and paintings. Jaime describes himself as loyal, hard-working and dedicated.